Music Minus One

4505

F.A. Hoffmeister
Concerto in D major for Viola and Orchestra

Complete Version	Background Tracks	Movement Titles	Page No.
1	5	1st Mvt. Allegro	5
2	6	2nd Mvt. Adagio	9
3	7	3rd Mvt. Rondo	10
4		A 440 Tuning Notes	

Music Minus One • 50 Executive Boulevard • Elmsford, New York 10523-1325
Website: www.musicminusone.com   Phone: 914-592-1188 • Fax: 914-592-3575

Franz Hoffmeister
Concerto for Viola in D Major

Although the name of Franz Anton Hoffmeister is all but forgotten in musical circles and almost completely unknown to the public, he was a vital force in music during the late eighteenth and early nineteenth centuries. Born at Rotenburg-am-Neckar, in what is now Germany, on 12 May 1754, he quickly developed into a prolific composer, conductor and an eminent publisher who was vitally important in the Viennese music world. In fact, none other than Wolfgang Amadeus Mozart owed a good deal of his livelihood to Hoffmeister's generosity. It was Hoffmeister who underwrote much of Mozart's compositional activities, actively championing some of the young man's more unpopular works and publishing large amounts of his expanding *oeuvre,* as well as bankrolling him during hard times. Also, Hoffmeister was close friends with Haydn and, later, with Beethoven, whose friendship was strong enough to warrant Beethoven calling him "most beloved brother."

In 1800 the then-46-year-old impresario joined forces with organist and bookseller Ambrosius Kühnel (1770-1813) to expand his publishing business into a 'Bureau de Musique' in Leipzig. It was around this time that his friendship with Beethoven really blossomed, and the company became the publisher of that master's First Symphony and his Second Piano Concerto. This venture eventually became the famous firm of C. F. Peters, still one of the most regarded music publishers in the world.

But aside from this line of work, by the time of his death in 1812 he had written an almost unbelievable number of musical compositions, including almost 70 symphonies, about 500 chamber works, and 75 concerti, of which this viola concerto is his most lasting and prominent piece.

The viola had always taken a subsidiary role to the other stringed instruments, as it was perceived to have a far inferior tone, and this was reinforced by the wide variance in design which resulted in a glut of terrible instruments, and the large number of inferior players. It took adventurous composers like Mozart, who loved playing the instrument and wrote his wonderful *Sinfonia concertante,* and his friend Hoffmeister, to bring the instrument to a higher level of acceptance and to give the public an understanding of its uniquely beautiful capabilities.

Hoffmeister's concerto, scored for string orchestra, two oboes, and two french horns, opens with the strings prominently in *tutti* from the first bar. The solo instrument enters forcefully with a quadruple-stop and moves with virtuosity through a good deal of passagework to the cadenza.

The somber but beautiful *adagio* is carefully written to make display of the soulful quality which the viola possesses. Hoffmeister is careful to balance the viola's muted presence against an appropriately subdued orchestral accompaniment, using subtle techniques of contrast to effectively set the one against the many throughout the movement.

In the delicately energetic *rondo,* Hoffmeister mixes the dance-like rhythms with a certain piquancy which is very striking, at the same time bringing out the mellower tones of the viola most effectively, finishing the piece in a thoroughly engaging manner.

We can be grateful to Hoffmeister for leaving us this concerto, as it fills a need for a beautiful expression of what has surely been a very undervalued instrument in the concerto repertoire, especially during the classical period. While it would take Berlioz's *Harold in Italy* and high romanticism to finally give the instrument much of the respect it enjoys today, this concerto did no small part to pave the way.

—*Michael Norell*

F.A. Hoffmeister

Concerto for Viola and Orchestra
In D major

4505

Printed in Canada

Concerto for Viola and Orchestra

F. A. Hoffmeister

Viola Solo

(1754~1812)

Allegro

MMO 4505

Adagio

Solo

MMO Compact Disc Catalog

Bold Face Text = New Releases

BROADWAY

____	LES MISERABLES/PHANTOM OF THE OPERA	MMO CD 1016
____	HITS OF ANDREW LLOYD WEBBER	MMO CD 1054
____	GUYS AND DOLLS	MMO CD 1067
____	WEST SIDE STORY 2 CD Set	MMO CD 1100
____	CABARET 2 CD Set	MMO CD 1110
____	BROADWAY HEROES AND HEROINES	MMO CD 1121
____	CAMELOT	MMO CD 1173
____	BEST OF ANDREW LLOYD WEBBER	MMO CD 1130
____	THE SOUND OF BROADWAY	MMO CD 1133
____	BROADWAY MELODIES	MMO CD 1134
____	BARBRA'S BROADWAY	MMO CD 1144
____	JEKYLL & HYDE	MMO CD 1151
____	SHOWBOAT	MMO CD 1160
____	MY FAIR LADY 2 CD Set	MMO CD 1174
____	OKLAHOMA	MMO CD 1175
____	THE SOUND OF MUSIC 2 CD Set	MMO CD 1176
____	SOUTH PACIFIC	MMO CD 1177
____	THE KING AND I	MMO CD 1178
____	FIDDLER ON THE ROOF 2 CD Set	MMO CD 1179
____	CAROUSEL	MMO CD 1180
____	PORGY AND BESS	MMO CD 1181
____	THE MUSIC MAN	MMO CD 1183
____	ANNIE GET YOUR GUN 2 CD Set	MMO CD 1186
____	HELLO DOLLY! 2 CD Set	MMO CD 1187
____	OLIVER 2 CD Set	MMO CD 1189
____	SUNSET BOULEVARD	MMO CD 1193
____	GREASE	MMO CD 1196
____	SMOKEY JOE'S CAFE	MMO CD 1197
____	MISS SAIGON	MMO CD 1226
____	**THE SCARLET PIMPERNEL 2 CD Set**	**PSCDG 1389**
____	**RENT 2 CD Set**	**PSCD 1396**

CLARINET

____	MOZART CONCERTO, IN A, K.622	MMO CD 3201
____	WEBER CONCERTO NO. 1 in Fm. STAMITZ CONC. No. 3 IN Bb	MMO CD 3202
____	SPOHR CONCERTO NO. 1 IN C MINOR OP. 26	MMO CD 3203
____	WEBER CONCERTO OP. 26, BEETHOVEN TRIO OP. 11	MMO CD 3204
____	FIRST CHAIR CLARINET SOLOS	MMO CD 3205
____	THE ART OF THE SOLO CLARINET:	MMO CD 3206
____	MOZART QUINTET IN A, K.581	MMO CD 3207
____	BRAHMS SONATAS OP. 120 NO. 1 & 2	MMO CD 3208
____	WEBER GRAND DUO CONCERTANT WAGNER ADAGIO	MMO CD 3209
____	SCHUMANN FANTASY OP. 73, 3 ROMANCES OP. 94	MMO CD 3210
____	EASY CLARINET SOLOS Volume 1 - STUDENT LEVEL	MMO CD 3211
____	EASY CLARINET SOLOS Volume 2 - STUDENT LEVEL	MMO CD 3212
____	EASY JAZZ DUETS - STUDENT LEVEL	MMO CD 3213
____	VISIONS The Clarinet Artistry of Ron Odrich	MMO CD 3214
____	**IN A LEAGUE OF HIS OWN Popular Songs played by Ron Odrich and You**	**MMO CD 3215**
____	**SINATRA SET TO MUSIC Kern, Weill, Gershwin, Howard and You**	**MMO CD 3216**
____	**STRAVINSKY: L'HISTOIRE DU SOLDAT**	**MMO CD 3217**
____	**JAZZ STANDARDS with RHYTHM SECTION (2 CD Set)**	**MMO CD 3218**
____	**JAZZ STANDARDS WITH STRINGS (2 CD Set)**	**MMO CD 3219**
____	**RON ODRICH PLAYS STANDARDS**	**MMO CD 3220**
____	BEGINNING CONTEST SOLOS - Jerome Bunke, Clinician	MMO CD 3221
____	BEGINNING CONTEST SOLOS - Harold Wright	MMO CD 3222
____	INTERMEDIATE CONTEST SOLOS - Stanley Drucker	MMO CD 3223
____	INTERMEDIATE CONTEST SOLOS - Jerome Bunke, Clinician	MMO CD 3224
____	ADVANCED CONTEST SOLOS - Stanley Drucker	MMO CD 3225
____	ADVANCED CONTEST SOLOS - Harold Wright	MMO CD 3226
____	INTERMEDIATE CONTEST SOLOS - Stanley Drucker	MMO CD 3227
____	ADVANCED CONTEST SOLOS - Stanley Drucker	MMO CD 3228
____	ADVANCED CONTEST SOLOS - Harold Wright	MMO CD 3229
____	BRAHMS Clarinet Quintet in Bm, Op. 115	MMO CD 3230
____	TEACHER'S PARTNER Basic Clarinet Studies	MMO CD 3231
____	JEWELS FOR WOODWIND QUINTET	MMO CD 3232
____	WOODWIND QUINTETS minus CLARINET	MMO CD 3233
____	FROM DIXIE to SWING	MMO CD 3234
____	BEETHOVEN: QUINTET FOR CLARINET in Eb Major, Opus 16	MMO CD 3235
____	MOZART: QUINTET FOR CLARINET in Eb. K.452	MMO CD 3236
____	6 BANDS ON A HOT TIN ROOF New Swing for Trumpet	MMO CD 3237
____	THE VIRTUOSO CLARINETIST Baermann Method, Op. 63 4 CD Set	MMO CD 3240
____	ART OF THE CLARINET Baermann Method, Op. 64 4 CD Set	MMO CD 3241
____	POPULAR CONCERT FAVORITES WITH ORCHESTRA	MMO CD 3242
____	BAND-AIDS CONCERT BAND FAVORITES WITH ORCHESTRA	MMO CD 3243
____	WORLD FAVORITES Student Editions, 41 Easy Selections (1st-2nd year)	MMO CD 3244
____	CLASSIC THEMES Student Editions, 27 Easy Songs (2nd-3rd year)	MMO CD 3245

PIANO

____	BEETHOVEN CONCERTO NO. 1 IN C	MMO CD 3001
____	BEETHOVEN CONCERTO NO. 2 IN Bb	MMO CD 3002
____	BEETHOVEN CONCERTO NO. 3 IN C MINOR	MMO CD 3003
____	BEETHOVEN CONCERTO NO. 4 IN G	MMO CD 3004
____	BEETHOVEN CONCERTO NO. 5 IN Eb (2 CD SET)	MMO CD 3005
____	GRIEG CONCERTO IN A MINOR OP.16	MMO CD 3006
____	RACHMANINOFF CONCERTO NO. 2 IN C MINOR	MMO CD 3007
____	SCHUMANN CONCERTO IN A MINOR	MMO CD 3008
____	BRAHMS CONCERTO NO. 1 IN D MINOR (2 CD SET)	MMO CD 3009
____	CHOPIN CONCERTO NO. 1 IN E MINOR OP. 11	MMO CD 3010
____	MENDELSSOHN CONCERTO NO. 1 IN G MINOR	MMO CD 3011
____	MOZART CONCERTO NO. 9 IN Eb K.271	MMO CD 3012
____	MOZART CONCERTO NO. 12 IN A K.414	MMO CD 3013
____	MOZART CONCERTO NO. 20 IN D MINOR K.466	MMO CD 3014
____	MOZART CONCERTO NO. 23 IN A K.488	MMO CD 3015
____	MOZART CONCERTO NO. 24 IN C MINOR K.491	MMO CD 3016
____	MOZART CONCERTO NO. 26 IN D K.537, CORONATION	MMO CD 3017
____	MOZART CONCERTO NO. 17 IN G K.453	MMO CD 3018
____	LISZT CONCERTO NO. 1 IN Eb, WEBER OP. 79	MMO CD 3019
____	LISZT CONCERTO NO. 2 IN A, HUNGARIAN FANTASIA	MMO CD 3020
____	J.S. BACH CONCERTO IN F MINOR, J.C. BACH CON. IN Eb	MMO CD 3021
____	J.S. BACH CONCERTO IN D MINOR	MMO CD 3022
____	HAYDN CONCERTO IN D	MMO CD 3023
____	HEART OF THE PIANO CONCERTO	MMO CD 3024
____	THEMES FROM GREAT PIANO CONCERTI	MMO CD 3025
____	TSCHAIKOVSKY CONCERTO NO. 1 IN Bb MINOR	MMO CD 3026
____	ART OF POPULAR PIANO PLAYING, Vol. 1 STUDENT LEVEL	MMO CD 3033
____	ART OF POPULAR PIANO PLAYING, Vol. 2 STUDENT LEVEL 2 CD Set	MMO CD 3034
____	'POP' PIANO FOR STARTERS STUDENT LEVEL	MMO CD 3035
____	DVORAK TRIO IN A MAJOR, OP. 90 "Dumky Trio"	MMO CD 3037
____	DVORAK QUINTET IN A MAJOR, OP. 81	MMO CD 3038
____	MENDELSSOHN TRIO IN D MAJOR, OP. 49	MMO CD 3039
____	MENDELSSOHN TRIO IN C MINOR, OP. 66	MMO CD 3040
____	BLUES FUSION FOR PIANO	MMO CD 3049
____	CLAUDE BOLLING SONATA FOR FLUTE AND JAZZ PIANO TRIO	MMO CD 3050
____	TWENTY DIXIELAND CLASSICS	MMO CD 3051
____	TWENTY RHYTHM BACKGROUNDS TO STANDARDS	MMO CD 3052
____	FROM DIXIE to SWING	MMO CD 3053
____	J.S. BACH BRANDENBURG CONCERTO NO. 5 IN D MAJOR	MMO CD 3054
____	BACH Cm CONC. - 2 PIANOS / SCHUMANN & VAR., OP. 46 - 2 PIANOS	MMO CD 3055
____	J.C. BACH Bm CONC./HAYDN C CONCERT./HANDEL CONC. GROSSO-D	MMO CD 3056
____	J.S. BACH TRIPLE CONCERTO IN A MINOR	MMO CD 3057
____	FRANCK SYM. VAR. / MENDELSSOHN: CAPRICCO BRILLANT	MMO CD 3058
____	C.P.E. BACH CONCERTO IN A MINOR	MMO CD 3059
____	STRETCHIN' OUT-'Comping' with a Jazz Rhythm Section	MMO CD 3060
____	**RAVEL: PIANO TRIO**	**MMO CD 3061**
____	**THE JIM ODRICH EXPERIENCE Pop Piano Played Easy**	**MMO CD 3062**
____	**POPULAR PIANO MADE EASY Arranged by Jim Odrich**	**MMO CD 3063**
____	**SCHUMANN: Piano Trio in D Minor, Opus 63**	**MMO CD 3064**
____	**BEETHOVEN: Trio No. 8 & Trio No. 11, "Kakadu" Variations**	**MMO CD 3065**
____	**SCHUBERT: Piano Trio in Bb Major, Opus 99 (2 CD Set)**	**MMO CD 3066**
____	**SCHUBERT: Piano Trio in Eb Major, Opus 100 (2 CD Set)**	**MMO CD 3067**
____	**SCHUBERT: Piano Trio in Eb Major, Opus 100 (2 CD Set)**	**MMO CD 3068**
____	**POPULAR SONGS Arranged by Jim Odrich**	**MMO CD 3069**
____	**BEETHOVEN: QUINTET FOR PIANO in Eb Major, Opus 16**	**MMO CD 3070**
____	**MOZART: QUINTET FOR PIANO in Eb, K.452**	**MMO CD 3071**
____	**MOZART: PIANO CONCERTO #21 IN C MAJOR, K.467**	**MMO CD 3072**
____	**MOZART: PIANO CONCERTO KV 449.**	**MMO CD 3073**
____	**CHOPIN: PIANO CONCERTO in F minor, Opus 21.**	**MMO CD 3074**
____	**RACHMANINOV: CONCERTO NO.3 in D minor.**	**MMO CD 3075**
____	**HAYDN: Trios in F#, F and G.**	**MMO CD 3076**

PIANO - FOUR HANDS

____	RACHMANINOFF Six Scenes.....4-5th year	MMO CD 3027
____	ARENSKY 6 Pieces, STRAVINSKY 3 Easy Dances...2-3rd year	MMO CD 3028
____	FAURE: The Dolly Suite	MMO CD 3029
____	DEBUSSY: Four Pieces	MMO CD 3030
____	SCHUMANN Pictures from the East.....4-5th year	MMO CD 3031
____	BEETHOVEN Three Marches.....4-5th year	MMO CD 3032
____	MOZART COMPLETE MUSIC FOR PIANO FOUR HANDS 2 CD Set	MMO CD 3036
____	MAYKAPAR First Steps, OP. 29.....1-2nd year	MMO CD 3041
____	TSCHAIKOVSKY: 50 Russian Folk Songs	MMO CD 3042
____	BIZET: 12 Children's Games	MMO CD 3043
____	GRETCHANINOFF: ON THE GREEN MEADOW	MMO CD 3044
____	POZZOLI: SMILES OF CHILDHOOD	MMO CD 3045
____	DIABELLI: PLEASURES OF YOUTH	MMO CD 3046
____	SCHUBERT: FANTASIA & GRAND SONATA	MMO CD 3047

MMO Music Group • 50 Executive Boulevard, Elmsford, New York 10523, 1-(800) 669-7464
Website: www. minusone.com • E-mail: mmomus@aol.com

MMO Compact Disc Catalog

Bold Face Text = New Releases—*—In Preparation

VIOLIN

- BRUCH CONCERTO NO. 1 IN G MINOR OP.26 ... MMO CD 3100
- MENDELSSOHN CONCERTO IN E MINOR ... MMO CD 3101
- TSCHAIKOVSKY CONCERTO IN D OP. 35 ... MMO CD 3102
- BACH DOUBLE CONCERTO IN D MINOR ... MMO CD 3103
- BACH CONCERTO IN A MINOR, CONCERTO IN E ... MMO CD 3104
- BACH BRANDENBURG CONCERTI NOS. 4 & 5 ... MMO CD 3105
- BACH BRANDENBURG CONCERTO NO. 2,TRIPLE CONCERTO ... MMO CD 3106
- BACH CONCERTO IN DM, (FROM CONCERTO FOR HARPSICHORD) ... MMO CD 3107
- BRAHMS CONCERTO IN D OP. 77 ... MMO CD 3108
- CHAUSSON POEME, SCHUBERT RONDO ... MMO CD 3109
- LALO SYMPHONIE ESPAGNOLE ... MMO CD 3110
- MOZART CONCERTO IN D K.218, VIVALDI CON. AM OP.3 NO.6 ... MMO CD 3111
- MOZART CONCERTO IN A K.219 ... MMO CD 3112
- WIENIAWSKI CON. IN D. SARASATE ZIGEUNERWEISEN ... MMO CD 3113
- VIOTTI CONCERTO NO. 22 IN A MINOR ... MMO CD 3114
- BEETHOVEN 2 ROMANCES, SONATA NO. 5 IN F "SPRING SONATA" ... MMO CD 3115
- SAINT-SAENS INTRODUCTION & RONDO, MOZART SERENADE K. 204, ADAGIO K.261 ... MMO CD 3116
- BEETHOVEN CONCERTO IN D OP. 61(2 CD SET) ... MMO CD 3117
- THE CONCERTMASTER - Orchestral Excerpts ... MMO CD 3118
- AIR ON A G STRING Favorite Encores with Orchestra Easy Medium ... MMO CD 3119
- CONCERT PIECES FOR THE SERIOUS VIOLINIST Easy Medium ... MMO CD 3120
- 18TH CENTURY VIOLIN PIECES ... MMO CD 3121
- ORCHESTRAL FAVORITES - Volume 1 - Easy Level ... MMO CD 3122
- ORCHESTRAL FAVORITES - Volume 2 - Medium Level ... MMO CD 3123
- ORCHESTRAL FAVORITES - Volume 3 - Med to Difficult Level ... MMO CD 3124
- THE THREE B'S BACH/BEETHOVEN/BRAHMS ... MMO CD 3125
- VIVALDI: VIOLIN CONCERTOS ... MMO CD 3126
- VIVALDI-THE FOUR SEASONS (2 CD Set) ... MMO CD 3127
- VIVALDI Concerto in Eb, Op. 8, No. 5. ALBINONI Concerto in A ... MMO CD 3128
- VIVALDI Concerto in E, Op. 3, No. 12. Concerto in C Op. 8, No.6 "Il Piacere" MMO CD 3129
- SCHUBERT Three Sonatinas ... MMO CD 3130
- HAYDN String Quartet Op. 76 No. 1 ... MMO CD 3131
- HAYDN String Quartet Op. 76 No. 2 ... MMO CD 3132
- HAYDN String Quartet Op. 76 No. 3 "Emperor" ... MMO CD 3133
- HAYDN String Quartet Op. 76 No. 4 "Sunrise" ... MMO CD 3134
- HAYDN String Quartet Op. 76 No. 5 ... MMO CD 3135
- HAYDN String Quartet Op. 76 No. 6 ... MMO CD 3136
- BEAUTIFUL MUSIC FOR TWO VIOLINS 1st position, vol. 1 ... MMO CD 3137«
- BEAUTIFUL MUSIC FOR TWO VIOLINS 2nd position, vol. 2 ... MMO CD 3138«
- BEAUTIFUL MUSIC FOR TWO VIOLINS 3rd position, vol. 3 ... MMO CD 3139«
- BEAUTIFUL MUSIC FOR TWO VIOLINS 1st, 2nd, 3rd position, vol. 4 ... MMO CD 3140«

«Lovely folk tunes and selections from the classics, chosen for their melodic beauty and technical value. They have been skillfully transcribed and edited by Samuel Applebaum, one of America's foremost teachers.

- HEART OF THE VIOLIN CONCERTO ... MMO CD 3141
- TEACHER'S PARTNER Basic Violin Studies 1st year ... MMO CD 3142
- DVORAK STRING TRIO "Terzetto", OP. 74 2 violins/viola ... MMO CD 3143
- SIBELIUS: Concerto in D minor, Op. 47 ... MMO CD 3144
- THEMES FROM THE MAJOR VIOLIN CONCERTI ... MMO CD 3145
- STRAVINSKY: L'HISTOIRE DU SOLDAT ... MMO CD 3146
- RAVEL: PIANO TRIO MINUS VIOLIN ... MMO CD 3147
- GREAT VIOLIN MOMENTS ... MMO CD 3148
- RAGTIME STRING QUARTETS The Zinn String Quartet ... MMO CD 3151
- SCHUMANN: Piano Trio in D minor, Opus 63 ... MMO CD 3152
- BEETHOVEN: Trio No. 8 & Trio No. 11, "Kakadu" Variations ... MMO CD 3153
- SCHUBERT: Piano Trio in Bb Major, Opus 99 Minus Violin (2 CD Set) ... MMO CD 3154
- SCHUBERT: Piano Trio in Eb Major, Opus 100 Minus Violin (2 CD Set) ... MMO CD 3155
- BEETHOVEN: STRING QUARTET in A minor, Opus 132 (2 CD Set) ... MMO CD 3156
- DVORAK QUINTET in A major, Opus 81 Minus Violin ... MMO CD 3157
- BEETHOVEN: STRING QTS No. 1 in F major & No. 4 in C minor, Opus 18 ... MMO CD 3158
- HAYDN Three Trios with Piano & Cello ... MMO CD 3159
- **MOZART: CONCERTO NO. 3 FOR VIOLIN AND ORCHESTRA. ... MMO CD 3160**
- MISCHA ELMAN FAVORITE ENCORES. ... MMO CD 3162
- MISCHA ELMAN CONCERT FAVORITES ... MMO CD 3163
- JASCHA HEIFETZ FAVORITE ENCORES. ... MMO CD 3164
- FRITZ KREISLER FAVORITE ENCORES ... MMO CD 3165

GUITAR

- BOCCHERINI Quintet No. 4 in D "Fandango" ... MMO CD 3601
- GIULIANI Quintet in A Op. 65 ... MMO CD 3602
- CLASSICAL GUITAR DUETS ... MMO CD 3603
- RENAISSANCE & BAROQUE GUITAR DUETS ... MMO CD 3604
- CLASSICAL & ROMANTIC GUITAR DUETS ... MMO CD 3605
- GUITAR AND FLUTE DUETS Volume 1 ... MMO CD 3606
- GUITAR AND FLUTE DUETS Volume 2 ... MMO CD 3607
- BLUEGRASS GUITAR ... MMO CD 3608
- GEORGE BARNES GUITAR METHOD Lessons from a Master ... MMO CD 3609
- HOW TO PLAY FOLK GUITAR 2 CD Set ... MMO CD 3610
- FAVORITE FOLKS SONGS FOR GUITAR ... MMO CD 3611
- FOR GUITARS ONLY! Jimmy Raney Small Band Arrangements ... MMO CD 3612
- TEN DUETS FOR TWO GUITARS Geo. Barnes/Carl Kress ... MMO CD 3613
- PLAY THE BLUES GUITAR A Dick Weissman Method ... MMO CD 3614
- **ORCHESTRAL GEMS FOR CLASSICAL GUITAR ... MMO CD 3615**

FLUTE

- MOZART Concerto No. 2 in D, QUANTZ Concerto in G ... MMO CD 3300
- MOZART Concerto in G K.313 ... MMO CD 3301
- BACH Suite No. 2 in B Minor ... MMO CD 3302
- BOCCHERINI Concerto in D, VIVALDI Concerto in G Minor "La Notte", MOZART Andante for Strings ... MMO CD 3303
- HAYDN Divertimento, VIVALDI Concerto in D Op. 10 No. 3 "Bullfinch", FREDERICK THE GREAT Concerto in C ... MMO CD 3304
- VIVALDI Conc. in F; TELEMANN Conc. in D; LECLAIR Conc. in C ... MMO CD 3305
- BACH Brandenburg No. 2 in F, HAYDN Concerto in D ... MMO CD 3306
- BACH Triple Concerto, VIVALDI Concerto in D Minor ... MMO CD 3307
- MOZART Quartet in F, STAMITZ Quartet in F ... MMO CD 3308
- HAYDN 4 London Trios for 2 Flutes & Cello ... MMO CD 3309
- BACH Brandenburg Concerti Nos. 4 & 5 ... MMO CD 3310
- MOZART 3 Flute Quartets in D, A and C ... MMO CD 3311
- TELEMANN Suite in A Minor, GLUCK Scene from 'Orpheus', PERGOLESI Concerto in G (2 CD Set) ... MMO CD 3312
- FLUTE SONG: Easy Familiar Classics ... MMO CD 3313
- VIVALDI Concerti In D, G, and F ... MMO CD 3314
- VIVALDI Concerti in A Minor, G, and D ... MMO CD 3315
- EASY FLUTE SOLOS Beginning Students Volume 1 ... MMO CD 3316
- EASY FLUTE SOLOS Beginning Students Volume 2 ... MMO CD 3317
- EASY JAZZ DUETS Student Level ... MMO CD 3318
- FLUTE & GUITAR DUETS Volume 1 ... MMO CD 3319
- FLUTE & GUITAR DUETS Volume 2 ... MMO CD 3320
- BEGINNING CONTEST SOLOS Murray Panitz ... MMO CD 3321
- BEGINNING CONTEST SOLOS Donald Peck ... MMO CD 3322
- INTERMEDIATE CONTEST SOLOS Julius Baker ... MMO CD 3323
- INTERMEDIATE CONTEST SOLOS Donald Peck ... MMO CD 3324
- ADVANCED CONTEST SOLOS Murray Panitz ... MMO CD 3325
- ADVANCED CONTEST SOLOS Julius Baker ... MMO CD 3326
- INTERMEDIATE CONTEST SOLOS Donald Peck ... MMO CD 3327
- ADVANCED CONTEST SOLOS Murray Panitz ... MMO CD 3328
- ADVANCED CONTEST SOLOS Julius Baker ... MMO CD 3329
- BEGINNING CONTEST SOLOS Doriot Anthony Dwyer ... MMO CD 3330
- INTERMEDIATE CONTEST SOLOS Doriot Anthony Dwyer ... MMO CD 3331
- ADVANCED CONTEST SOLOS Doriot Anthony Dwyer ... MMO CD 3332
- FIRST CHAIR SOLOS with Orchestral Accompaniment ... MMO CD 3333
- TEACHER'S PARTNER Basic Flute Studies 1st year ... MMO CD 3334
- THE JOY OF WOODWIND MUSIC ... MMO CD 3335
- JEWELS FOR WOODWIND QUINTET ... MMO CD 3336
- TELEMANN TRIO IN F/Bb MAJOR/HANDEL SON.#3 IN C MAJOR ... MMO CD 3340
- MARCELLO/TELEMANN/HANDEL SONATAS IN F MAJOR ... MMO CD 3341
- BOLLING: SUITE FOR FLUTE/JAZZ PIANO TRIO ... MMO CD 3342
- HANDEL / TELEMANN SIX SONATAS 2 CD Set ... MMO CD 3343
- BACH SONATA NO. 1 in B MINOR/KUHLAU E MINOR DUET (2 CD set) ... MMO CD 3344
- KUHLAU TRIO in Eb MAJOR/BACH Eb AND A MAJOR SONATA (2 CD set) .. MMO CD 3345
- PEPUSCH SONATA IN C / TELEMANN SONATA IN Cm ... MMO CD 3346
- QUANTZ TRIO SONATA IN Cm / BACH GIGUE / ABEL SON. 2 IN F ... MMO CD 3347
- TELEMANN CONCERTO NO. 1 IN D / CORRETTE SONATA IN E MINOR ... MMO CD 3348
- TELEMANN TRIO IN F / Bb MAJOR / HANDEL SON. #3 IN C MAJOR ... MMO CD 3349
- MARCELLO / TELEMANN / HANDEL SONATAS IN F MAJOR ... MMO CD 3350
- CONCERT BAND FAVORITES WITH ORCHESTRA ... MMO CD 3351
- BAND-AIDS CONCERT BAND FAVORITES WITH ORCHESTRA ... MMO CD 3352
- **WORLD FAVORITES Student Editions, 41 Easy Selections (1st-2nd year) MMO CD 3354**
- **CLASSIC THEMES Student Editions, 27 Easy Songs (2nd-3rd year) ... MMO CD 3355**

RECORDER

- PLAYING THE RECORDER Folk Songs of Many Nations ... MMO CD 3337
- LET'S PLAY THE RECORDER Beginning Children's Method ... MMO CD 3338
- YOU CAN PLAY THE RECORDER Beginning Adult Method ... MMO CD 3339

FRENCH HORN

- MOZART: Concerti No. 2 & No. 3 in Eb. K. 417 & 447 ... MMO CD 3501
- BAROQUE BRASS AND BEYOND ... MMO CD 3502
- MUSIC FOR BRASS ENSEMBLE ... MMO CD 3503
- MOZART: Sonatas for Two Horns ... MMO CD 3504
- BEETHOVEN: QUINTET FOR FRENCH HORN in Eb Major, Opus 16 ... MMO CD 3505
- MOZART: QUINTET FOR FRENCH HORN in Eb, K.452 ... MMO CD 3506
- BEGINNING CONTEST SOLOS Mason Jones ... MMO CD 3511
- BEGINNING CONTEST SOLOS Myron Bloom ... MMO CD 3512
- INTERMEDIATE CONTEST SOLOS Dale Clevenger ... MMO CD 3513
- INTERMEDIATE CONTEST SOLOS Mason Jones ... MMO CD 3514
- ADVANCED CONTEST SOLOS Myron Bloom ... MMO CD 3515

MMO Music Group • 50 Executive Boulevard, Elmsford, New York 10523, 1-(800) 669-7464
Website: www. minusone.com • E-mail: mmomus@aol.com

MMO Compact Disc Catalog

_____ADVANCED CONTEST SOLOS Dale Clevenger.................

_____ INTERMEDIATE CONTEST SOLOS Mason Jones ....MMO CD 3517
_____ ADVANCED CONTEST SOLOS Myron Bloom ....MMO CD 3518
_____ INTERMEDIATE CONTEST SOLOS Dale Clevenger ....MMO CD 3519
_____ FRENCH HORN WOODWIND MUSIC ....MMO CD 3520
_____ MASTERPIECES FOR WOODWIND QUINTET ....MMO CD 3521
_____ FRENCH HORN UP FRONT BRASS QUINTETS ....MMO CD 3522
_____ HORN OF PLENTY BRASS QUINTETS ....MMO CD 3523
_____ BAND-AIDS CONCERT BAND FAVORITES WITH ORCHESTRA ....MMO CD 3524

TRUMPET

_____ THREE CONCERTI: HAYDN, TELEMANN, FASCH ....MMO CD 3801
_____ TRUMPET SOLOS Student Level Volume 1 ....MMO CD 3802
_____ TRUMPET SOLOS Student Level Volume 2 ....MMO CD 3803
_____ EASY JAZZ DUETS Student Level ....MMO CD 3804
_____ MUSIC FOR BRASS ENSEMBLE Brass Quintets ....MMO CD 3805
_____ FIRST CHAIR TRUMPET SOLOS with Orchestral Accompaniment ....MMO CD 3806
_____ THE ART OF THE SOLO TRUMPET with Orchestral Accompaniment ....MMO CD 3807
_____ BAROQUE BRASS AND BEYOND Brass Quintets ....MMO CD 3808
_____ THE COMPLETE ARBAN DUETS all of the classic studies........MMO CD 3809
_____ SOUSA MARCHES PLUS BEETHOVEN, BERLIOZ, STRAUSS .....MMO CD 3810
_____ BEGINNING CONTEST SOLOS Gerard Schwarz ....MMO CD 3811
_____ BEGINNING CONTEST SOLOS Armando Ghitalla ....MMO CD 3812
_____ INTERMEDIATE CONTEST SOLOS Robert Nagel, Soloist ....MMO CD 3813
_____ INTERMEDIATE CONTEST SOLOS Gerard Schwarz ....MMO CD 3814
_____ ADVANCED CONTEST SOLOS Robert Nagel, Soloist ....MMO CD 3815
_____ CONTEST SOLOS Armando Ghitalla ....MMO CD 3816
_____ INTERMEDIATE CONTEST SOLOS Gerard Schwarz ....MMO CD 3817
_____ ADVANCED CONTEST SOLOS Robert Nagel, Soloist ....MMO CD 3818
_____ ADVANCED CONTEST SOLOS Armando Ghilalla ....MMO CD 3819
_____ BEGINNING CONTEST SOLOS Raymond Crisara ....MMO CD 3820
_____ BEGINNING CONTEST SOLOS Raymond Crisara ....MMO CD 3821
_____ INTERMEDIATE CONTEST SOLOS Raymond Crisara ....MMO CD 3822
_____ TEACHER'S PARTNER Basic Trumpet Studies 1st year ....MMO CD 3823
_____ TWENTY DIXIELAND CLASSICS ....MMO CD 3824
_____ TWENTY RHYTHM BACKGROUNDS TO STANDARDS ....MMO CD 3825
_____ FROM DIXIE TO SWING ....MMO CD 3826
_____ TRUMPET PIECES BRASS QUINTETS ....MMO CD 3827
_____ MODERN BRASS QUINTETS ....MMO CD 3828
_____ WHEN JAZZ WAS YOUNG The Bob Wilber All Stars ....MMO CD 3829
_____ CLASSIC TRUMPET SELECTIONS WITH PIANO ....MMO CD 3830
_____ CONCERT BAND FAVORITES WITH ORCHESTRA ....MMO CD 3831
_____ BAND-AIDS CONCERT BAND FAVORITES WITH ORCHESTRA ....MMO CD 3832
_____ **BRASS TRAX The Trumpet Artistry Of David O'Neill** ......**MMO CD 3833**
_____ **TRUMPET TRIUMPHANT The Further Adventures Of David O'Neill** ....**MMO CD 3834**
_____ **STRAVINSKY: L'HISTOIRE DU SOLDAT** ....**MMO CD 3835**
_____ WORLD FAVORITES Student Editions, 41 Easy Selections (1st-2nd year) MMO CD 3836
_____ CLASSIC THEMES Student Editions, 27 Easy Songs (2nd-3rd year) ....MMO CD 3837
_____ 6 BANDS ON A HOT TIN ROOF New Swing for Trumpet ....MMO CD 3838
_____ **12 CLASSIC JAZZ STANDARDS Bb/Eb/Bass Clef** ....**MMO CD 7010**
_____ **12 MORE CLASSIC JAZZ STANDARDS Bb/Eb/Bass Clef** ....**MMO CD 7011**

TROMBONE

_____ TROMBONE SOLOS Student Level Volume 1 ....MMO CD 3901
_____ TROMBONE SOLOS Student Level Volume 2 ....MMO CD 3902
_____ EASY JAZZ DUETS Student Level ....MMO CD 3903
_____ BAROQUE BRASS & BEYOND Brass Quintets....................MMO CD 3904
_____ MUSIC FOR BRASS ENSEMBLE Brass Quintets ....MMO CD 3905
_____ UNSUNG HERO George Roberts ....MMO CD 3906
_____ BIG BAND BALLADS George Roberts ....MMO CD 3907
_____ STRAVINSKY: L'HISTOIRE DU SOLDAT ....MMO CD 3908
_____ **CLASSICAL TROMBONE SOLOS** ....**MMO CD 3909**
_____ **JAZZ STANDARDS WITH STRINGS (2 CD Set)** ....**MMO CD 3910**
_____ BEGINNING CONTEST SOLOS Per Brevig ....MMO CD 3911
_____ BEGINNING CONTEST SOLOS Jay Friedman......................MMO CD 3912
_____ INTERMEDIATE CONTEST SOLOS Keith Brown, Professor, Indiana U. ....MMO CD 3913
_____ INTERMEDIATE CONTEST SOLOS Jay Friedman ....MMO CD 3914
_____ ADVANCED CONTEST SOLOS Keith Brown, Professor, Indiana University ..MMO CD 3915
_____ ADVANCED CONTEST SOLOS Per Brevig ....MMO CD 3916
_____ ADVANCED CONTEST SOLOS Keith Brown, Professor, Indiana University ..MMO CD 3917
_____ ADVANCED CONTEST SOLOS Jay Friedman ....MMO CD 3918
_____ ADVANCED CONTEST SOLOS Per Brevig ....MMO CD 3919
_____ TEACHER'S PARTNER Basic Trombone Studies 1st year ......MMO CD 3920
_____ TWENTY DIXIELAND CLASSICS ....MMO CD 3924
_____ TWENTY RHYTHM BACKGROUNDS TO STANDARDS ....MMO CD 3925
_____ FROM DIXIE TO SWING ....MMO CD 3926
_____ STICKS & BONES BRASS QUINTETS ....MMO CD 3927
_____ FOR TROMBONES ONLY MORE BRASS QUINTETS ....MMO CD 3928
_____ POPULAR CONCERT FAVORITES The Stuttgart Festival Band ....MMO CD 3929
_____ BAND-AIDS CONCERT BAND FAVORITES WITH ORCHESTRA ....MMO CD 3930
_____ WORLD FAVORITES Student Editions, 41 Easy Selections (1st-2nd year) MMO CD 3931

_____ CLASSIC THEMES Student Editions, 27 Easy Songs (2nd-3rd year) ....MMO CD 3932
_____ **12 CLASSIC JAZZ STANDARDS Bb/Eb/Bass Clef** ....**MMO CD 7010**
_____ **12 MORE CLASSIC JAZZ STANDARDS Bb/Eb/Bass Clef** ....**MMO CD 7011**

TENOR SAXOPHONE

_____ TENOR SAXOPHONE SOLOS Student Edition Volume 1 ......MMO CD 4201
_____ TENOR SAXOPHONE SOLOS Student Edition Volume 2 ......MMO CD 4202
_____ EASY JAZZ DUETS FOR TENOR SAXOPHONE ....MMO CD 4203
_____ FOR SAXES ONLY Arranged by Bob Wilber......................MMO CD 4204
_____ BLUES FUSION FOR SAXOPHONE ....MMO CD 4205
_____ JOBIM BRAZILIAN BOSSA NOVAS with STRINGS ....MMO CD 4206
_____ TWENTY DIXIE CLASSICS ....MMO CD 4207
_____ TWENTY RHYTHM BACKGROUNDS TO STANDARDS ....MMO CD 4208
_____ PLAY LEAD IN A SAX SECTION ....MMO CD 4209
_____ DAYS OF WINE & ROSES Sax Section Minus You ....MMO CD 4210
_____ FRENCH & AMERICAN SAXOPHONE QUARTETS ....MMO CD 4211
_____ CONCERT BAND FAVORITES WITH ORCHESTRA ....MMO CD 4212
_____ BAND AIDS CONCERT BAND FAVORITES ....MMO CD 4213
_____ **JAZZ JAM FOR TENOR (2 CD Set)** ....**MMO CD 4214**
_____ 6 BANDS ON A HOT TIN ROOF New Swing for Saxophone ....MMO CD 4215
_____ **12 CLASSIC JAZZ STANDARDS Bb/Eb/Bass Clef** ....**MMO CD 7010**
_____ **12 MORE CLASSIC JAZZ STANDARDS Bb/Eb/Bass Clef** ....**MMO CD 7011**

CELLO

_____ DVORAK Concerto in B Minor Op. 104 (2 CD Set) ....MMO CD 3701
_____ C.P.E. BACH Concerto in A Minor ....MMO CD 3702
_____ BOCCHERINI Concerto in Bb, BRUCH Kol Nidrei ....MMO CD 3703
_____ TEN PIECES FOR CELLO ....MMO CD 3704
_____ SCHUMANN Concerto in Am & Other Selections ....MMO CD 3705
_____ CLAUDE BOLLING Suite For Cello & Jazz Piano Trio ....MMO CD 3706
_____ RAVEL: PIANO TRIO MINUS CELLO ....MMO CD 3707
_____ **RAGTIME STRING QUARTETS** ....**MMO CD 3708**
_____ SCHUMANN: Piano Trio in D Minor, Opus 63 ....**MMO CD 3709**
_____ BEETHOVEN: Piano Trios No. 8 and 11 "Kakadu" ....**MMO CD 3710**
_____ SCHUBERT: Piano Trio in Bb Major, Opus 99 (2 CD Set) ....**MMO CD 3711**
_____ SCHUBERT: Piano Trio in Eb Major, Opus 100 (2 CD Set).....**MMO CD 3712**
_____ BEETHOVEN: STRING QUARTET in A minor, Opus 132 (2 CD Set) ....**MMO CD 3713**
_____ DVORAK QUINTET in A Major, Opus 81 ....**MMO CD 3714**
_____ BEETHOVEN: Sonata in A Major, Opus 69. ....**MMO CD 3715**
_____ WINER: Concerto/SCHUBERT: Ave Maria/SAINT-SAENS: Allegro Appass...MMO CD 3716

OBOE

_____ ALBINONI Concerti in Bb, Op. 7 No. 3, No. 6, D. Op. 9 No. 2 in Dm ....MMO CD 3400
_____ TELEMANN Conc. in Fm; HANDEL Conc. in Bb; VIVALDI Conc.in Dm ....MMO CD 3401
_____ MOZART Quartet in F K.370, STAMITZ Quartet in F Op. 8 No. 3 ....MMO CD 3402
_____ BACH Brandenburg Concerto No. 2, Telemann Con. in Am ....MMO CD 3403
_____ CLASSIC SOLOS FOR OBOE Delia Montenegro, Soloist ....MMO CD 3404
_____ MASTERPIECES FOR WOODWIND QUINTET ....MMO CD 3405
_____ THE JOY OF WOODWIND QUINTETS..................................MMO CD 3406
_____ PEPUSCH SONATAS IN C/TELEMANN SONATA IN Cm ....MMO CD 3407
_____ QUANTZ TRIO SONATA IN Cm/BACH GIGUE/ABEL SONATAS IN F ....MMO CD 3408
_____ **BEETHOVEN: QUINTET FOR OBOE in Eb, Opus 16** ....**MMO CD 3409**

ALTO SAXOPHONE

_____ ALTO SAXOPHONE SOLOS Student Edition Volume 1 ....MMO CD 4101
_____ ALTO SAXOPHONE SOLOS Student Edition Volume 2. ......MMO CD 4102
_____ EASY JAZZ DUETS FOR ALTO SAXOPHONE ....MMO CD 4103
_____ FOR SAXES ONLY Arranged Bob Wilber ....MMO CD 4104
_____ JOBIM BRAZILIAN BOSSA NOVAS with STRINGS ....MMO CD 4106
_____ UNSUNG HEROES FOR ALTO SAXOPHONE. ....MMO CD 4107
_____ 6 BANDS ON A HOT TIN ROOF New Swing for Trumpet ....MMO CD 4108
_____ BEGINNING CONTEST SOLOS Paul Brodie, Canadian Soloist ....MMO CD 4111
_____ BEGINNING CONTEST SOLOS Vincent Abato ....MMO CD 4112
_____ INTERMEDIATE CONTEST SOLOS Paul Brodie, Canadian Soloist ....MMO CD 4113
_____ INTERMEDIATE CONTEST SOLOS Vincent Abato ....MMO CD 4114
_____ ADVANCED CONTEST SOLOS Paul Brodie, Canadian Soloist...........MMO CD 4115
_____ ADVANCED CONTEST SOLOS Vincent Abato ....MMO CD 4116
_____ ADVANCED CONTEST SOLOS Paul Brodie, Canadian Soloist ....MMO CD 4117
_____ Basic Studies for Alto Sax TEACHER'S PARTNER 1st year level ....MMO CD 4119
_____ ADVANCED CONTEST SOLOS Vincent Abato ....MMO CD 4118
_____ PLAY LEAD IN A SAX SECTION ....MMO CD 4120
_____ DAYS OF WINE & ROSES/SENSUAL SAX ....MMO CD 4121
_____ TWENTY DIXIELAND CLASSICS ....MMO CD 4124
_____ TWENTY RHYTHM BACKGROUNDS TO STANDARDS ....MMO CD 4125
_____ CONCERT BAND FAVORITES WITH ORCHESTRA ....MMO CD 4126
_____ BAND AIDS CONCERT BAND FAVORITES ....MMO CD 4127
_____ **MUSIC FOR SAXOPHONE QUARTET.** ....**MMO CD 4128**

MMO Music Group • 50 Executive Boulevard, Elmsford, New York 10523, 1-(800) 669-7464
Website: www. minusone.com • E-mail: mmomus@aol.com

MMO Compact Disc Catalog

Bold Face Text = New Releases   * = In Preparation

___ WORLD FAVORITES Student Editions, 41 Easy Selections (1st-2nd year) MMO CD 4129
___ CLASSIC THEMES Student Editions, 27 Easy Songs (2nd-3rd year) ....MMO CD 4130
___ 6 BANDS ON A HOT TIN ROOF The New Swing Bands ....MMO CD 4131
___ GLAZUNOV: Concerto in Eb, Op.109 ....MMO CD 4132
___ 12 CLASSIC JAZZ STANDARDS Bb/Eb/Bass Clef ....MMO CD 7010
___ 12 MORE CLASSIC JAZZ STANDARDS Bb/Eb/Bass Clef ....MMO CD 7011

SOPRANO SAXOPHONE

___ FRENCH & AMERICAN SAXOPHONE QUARTETS ....MMO CD 4801
*___ 6 BANDS ON A HOT TIN ROOF New Swing for Trumpet ....MMO CD 4802
___ 12 CLASSIC JAZZ STANDARDS Bb/Eb/Bass Clef ....MMO CD 7010
___ 12 MORE CLASSIC JAZZ STANDARDS Bb/Eb/Bass Clef ....MMO CD 7011

BARITONE SAXOPHONE

___ MUSIC FOR SAXOPHONE QUARTET ....MMO CD 4901
*___ 6 BANDS ON A HOT TIN ROOF New Swing for Trumpet ....MMO CD 4902
___ 12 CLASSIC JAZZ STANDARDS Bb/Eb/Bass Clef ....MMO CD 7010
___ 12 MORE CLASSIC JAZZ STANDARDS Bb/Eb/Bass Clef ....MMO CD 7011

VOCAL

___ SCHUBERT GERMAN LIEDER - High Voice, Volume 1 ....MMO CD 4001
___ SCHUBERT GERMAN LIEDER - Low Voice, Volume 1 ....MMO CD 4002
___ SCHUBERT GERMAN LIEDER - High Voice, Volume 2 ....MMO CD 4003
___ SCHUBERT GERMAN LIEDER - Low Voice, Volume 2 ....MMO CD 4004
___ BRAHMS GERMAN LIEDER - High Voice ....MMO CD 4005
___ BRAHMS GERMAN LIEDER - Low Voice ....MMO CD 4006
___ EVERYBODY'S FAVORITE SONGS - High Voice, Volume 1 ....MMO CD 4007
___ EVERYBODY'S FAVORITE SONGS - Low Voice, Volume 1 ....MMO CD 4008
___ EVERYBODY'S FAVORITE SONGS - High Voice, Volume 2 ....MMO CD 4009
___ EVERYBODY'S FAVORITE SONGS - Low Voice, Volume 2 ....MMO CD 4010
___ 17th/18th CENT. ITALIAN SONGS - High Voice, Volume 1 ....MMO CD 4011
___ 17th/18th CENT. ITALIAN SONGS - Low Voice, Volume 1 ....MMO CD 4012
___ 17th/18th CENT. ITALIAN SONGS - High Voice, Volume 2 ....MMO CD 4013
___ 17th/18th CENT. ITALIAN SONGS - Low Voice, Volume 2 ....MMO CD 4014
___ FAMOUS SOPRANO ARIAS ....MMO CD 4015
___ FAMOUS MEZZO-SOPRANO ARIAS ....MMO CD 4016
___ FAMOUS TENOR ARIAS ....MMO CD 4017
___ FAMOUS BARITONE ARIAS..MMO CD 4018
___ FAMOUS BASS ARIAS ....MMO CD 4019
___ WOLF GERMAN LIEDER FOR HIGH VOICE ....MMO CD 4020
___ WOLF GERMAN LIEDER FOR LOW VOICE ....MMO CD 4021
___ STRAUSS GERMAN LIEDER FOR HIGH VOICE ....MMO CD 4022
___ STRAUSS GERMAN LIEDER FOR LOW VOICE ....MMO CD 4023
___ SCHUMANN GERMAN LIEDER FOR HIGH VOICE ....MMO CD 4024
___ SCHUMANN GERMAN LIEDER FOR LOW VOICE ....MMO CD 4025
___ MOZART ARIAS FOR SOPRANO ....MMO CD 4026
___ VERDI ARIAS FOR SOPRANO ....MMO CD 4027
___ ITALIAN ARIAS FOR SOPRANO ....MMO CD 4028
___ FRENCH ARIAS FOR SOPRANO ....MMO CD 4029
___ ORATORIO ARIAS FOR SOPRANO ....MMO CD 4030
___ ORATORIO ARIAS FOR ALTO ....MMO CD 4031
___ ORATORIO ARIAS FOR TENOR ....MMO CD 4032
___ ORATORIO ARIAS FOR BASS ....MMO CD 4033
___ BEGINNING SOPRANO SOLOS Kate Hurney ....MMO CD 4041
___ INTERMEDIATE SOPRANO SOLOS Kate Hurney ....MMO CD 4042
___ BEGINNING MEZZO SOPRANO SOLOS Fay Kittelson ....MMO CD 4043
___ INTERMEDIATE MEZZO SOPRANO SOLOS Fay Kittelson......................MMO CD 4044
___ ADVANCED MEZZO SOPRANO SOLOS Fay Kittelson ....MMO CD 4045
___ BEGINNING CONTRALTO SOLOS Carline Ray ....MMO CD 4046
___ BEGINNING TENOR SOLOS George Shirley ....MMO CD 4047
___ INTERMEDIATE TENOR SOLOS George Shirley ....MMO CD 4048
___ ADVANCED TENOR SOLOS George Shirley ....MMO CD 4049
___ TWELVE CLASSIC VOCAL STANDARDS, VOL.1 ....MMO CD 4050
___ TWELVE CLASSIC VOCAL STANDARDS, VOL.2 ....MMO CD 4051
___ SOPRANO ARIAS WITH ORCHESTRA ....MMO CD 4052
___ PUCCINI ARIAS FOR SOPRANO WITH ORCHESTRA ....MMO CD 4053
___ SOPRANO ARIAS WITH ORCHESTRA ....MMO CDG 4054
___ VERDI ARIAS FOR MEZZO-SOPRANO WITH ORCHESTRA ....MMO CDG 4055
___ BASS-BARITONE ARIAS WITH ORCHESTRA. ....MMO CDG 4056
___ ITALIAN TENOR ARIAS WITH ORCHESTRA ....MMO CDG 4057
___ DONIZETTI SOPRANO ARIAS WITH ORCHESTRA ....MMO CDG 4058
___ VERDI SOPRANO ARIAS WITH ORCHESTRA...MMO CD 4059

DOUBLE BASS

___ BEGINNING TO INTERMEDIATE CONTEST SOLOS David Walter ....MMO CD 4301
___ INTERMEDIATE TO ADVANCED CONTEST SOLOS David Walter ....MMO CD 4302
___ FOR BASSISTS ONLY Ken Smith, Soloist ....MMO CD 4303
___ THE BEAT GOES ON Jazz - Funk, Latin, Pop-Rock................................MMO CD 4304
___ FROM DIXIE TO SWING ....MMO CD 4305
___ STRAVINSKY: L'HISTOIRE DU SOLDAT ....MMO CD 4306

DRUMS

___ MODERN JAZZ DRUMMING 2 CD Set ....MMO CD 5001
___ FOR DRUMMERS ONLY...MMO CD 5002
___ WIPE OUT ....MMO CD 5003
___ SIT-IN WITH JIM CHAPIN ....MMO CD 5004
___ DRUM STAR Trios/Quartets/Quintets Minus You ....MMO CD 5005
___ DRUMPADSTICKSKIN Jazz play-alongs with small groups ....MMO CD 5006
___ JUMP & SWING DRUMS ....MMO CD 5007
___ CLASSICAL PERCUSSION 2 CD Set ....MMO CD 5009
___ EIGHT MEN IN SEARCH OF A DRUMMER ....MMO CD 5010
___ FROM DIXIE TO SWING ....MMO CD 5011
___ FABULOUS SOUNDS OF ROCK DRUMS ....MMO CD 5012
___ OPEN SESSION WITH THE GREG BURROWS QUINTET (2 CD Set)............MMO CD 5013
___ STRAVINSKY: L'HISTOIRE DU SOLDAT ....MMO CD 5014

VIOLA

___ VIOLA SOLOS with piano accompaniment ....MMO CD 4501
___ DVORAK STRING TRIO "Terzetto", OP. 74 2 Vlns/Viola ....MMO CD 4502
___ BEETHOVEN: STRING QUARTET in A minor, Opus 132 (2 CD Set) ....MMO CD 4503
___ DVORAK QUINTET in A major, Opus 81 Minus Viola...............................MMO CD 4504
___ VIOLA CONCERTI WITH ORCHESTRA J.C. Bach/j\Hofmaister ....MMO CD 4505

VIBES

___ FOR VIBISTS ONLY ....MMO CD 5101
___ GOOD VIB-RATIONS ....MMO CD 5102

BASSOON

___ SOLOS FOR THE BASSOON Janet Grice, Soloist ....MMO CD 4601
___ MASTERPIECES FOR WOODWIND MUSIC ....MMO CD 4602
___ THE JOY OF WOODWIND QUINTETS...MMO CD 4603
___ STRAVINSKY: L'HISTOIRE DU SOLDAT ....MMO CD 4604
___ BEETHOVEN: QUINTET FOR BASSOON in Eb, Opus 16.........................MMO CD 4605
___ MOZART: QUINTET FOR BASSOON in Eb, K.452 ....MMO CD 4606

BANJO

___ BLUEGRASS BANJO Classic & Favorite Banjo Pieces ....MMO CD 4401
___ PLAY THE FIVE STRING BANJO Vol. 1 Dick Weissman Method ....MMO CD 4402
___ PLAY THE FIVE STRING BANJO Vol. 2 Dick Weissman Method ....MMO CD 4403

TUBA or BASS TROMBONE

___ HE'S NOT HEAVY, HE'S MY TUBA ....MMO CD 4701
___ SWEETS FOR BRASS ....MMO CD 4702
___ MUSIC FOR BRASS ENSEMBLE ....MMO CD 4703

INSTRUCTIONAL METHODS

___ RUTGERS UNIVERSITY MUSIC DICTATION/EAR TRAINING (7 CD Set) ....MMO CD 7001
___ EVOLUTION OF THE BLUES ....MMO CD 7004
___ THE ART OF IMPROVISATION, VOL. 1 ....MMO CD 7005
___ THE ART OF IMPROVISATION, VOL. 2 ....MMO CD 7006
___ THE BLUES MINUS YOU Ed Xiques, Soloist..MMO CD 7007
___ TAKE A CHORUS minus Bb/Eb Instruments..MMO CD 7008
___ UNDERSTANDING JAZZ ....MMO CD 7009
___ 12 CLASSIC JAZZ STANDARDS Bb/Eb/Bass Clef ....MMO CD 7010
___ 12 MORE CLASSIC JAZZ STANDARDS Bb/Eb/Bass Clef ....MMO CD 7011

MMO Music Group • 50 Executive Boulevard, Elmsford, New York 10523, 1-(800) 669-7464
Website: www. minusone.com • E-mail: mmomus@aol.com

BUNGALOWS, CAMPS AND MOUNTAIN HOUSES

Bungalows, Camps and Mountain Houses

William Phillips Comstock and
Clarence Eaton Schermerhorn

Introduction by Tony P. Wrenn

Skyhorse Publishing

Skyhorse Publishing books may be purchased in bulk at special discounts for sales promotion, corporate gifts, fund-raising, or educational purposes. Special editions can also be created to specifications. For details, contact the Special Sales Department, Skyhorse Publishing, 307 West 36th Street, 11th Floor, New York, NY 10018 or info@skyhorsepublishing.com.

Skyhorse® and Skyhorse Publishing® are registered trademarks of Skyhorse Publishing, Inc.®, a Delaware corporation.

Visit our website at www.skyhorsepublishing.com.

10 9 8 7 6 5 4

Library of Congress Cataloging-in-Publication Data

Comstock, William Phillips.
  Bungalows, camps, and mountain houses / William Phillips Comstock and Clarence
Eaton Schermerhorn.
      p. cm.
  Reprint, with new introd. by Tony P. Wrenn. Originally published: Washington, D.C.
: W.T. Comstock, Co., c1908.
  ISBN-13: 978-1-60239-007-2 (pbk. : alk. paper)
  ISBN-10: 1-60239-007-X (pbk. : alk. paper)
  1. Vacation homes--United States--Designs and plans. 2. Cottages--United
States--Designs and plans. 3. Log cabins--United States--Designs and
plans. I.
Schermerhorn, Clarence Eaton, 1872-1925. II. Wrenn, Tony P. III. Title.

NA7575.C64 2007
728'.370222--dc22   2006038569

Printed in Canada

Contents

Bungalows: A Reintroduction, by Tony P. Wrenn   1

Preface to the 1915 Edition   25

Contributors   27

Introduction: The Bungalow   29

Planning the Bungalow, by C.E. Schermerhorn   33

Bungalows   41

Bungalows of Cottage Type   93

Camps, Lodges, Log Cabins   115

Bungalows: A Reintroduction

The bungalow may well be the quintessential American house of the early twentieth century. Transplanted from British India, the true bungalow is a one-story house with a low-pitched roof, often with multiple gables, wide roof overhang, and decoratively treated rafters. It generally features an open plan and several porches or verandas. Although the style was initially imported for vacation or summer houses, the flexibility of the plan quickly led to its adoption for year-round living. As builders and architects began to work with the bungalow, the house type became a national passion—the vacation home of the rich and the primary home of the average man. Literally no American suburb or street of the first quarter of this century is without its bungalow.

Although the bungalow was often built in the country as well, it is not to be confused with the cottage. Writing in 1901, R. A. Briggs handled the distinction with this neat turn of phrase: "A Cottage is a little house in the country, but a Bungalow is a little country house—a homely, cosy little place with verandahs and balconies and the plan so arranged as to ensure complete comfort, with a feeling of rusticity and ease."[1]

According to C. E. Schermerhorn, one of the authors of the volume reprinted here, more bungalows were erected and sold between 1909 and 1913 "than any other type of suburban dwelling." As he put it in a 1913 article in *Bungalow Magazine*, "[t]en years ago the automobile was scoffed at and the word 'bungalow' was pictured in the mind's eye as a hovel or shack along a waterfront or in some backwoods. But note the change in public opinion, as this type of house is now highly regarded by the homeseekers in every clime."[2] In fact, Schermerhorn noted that in suburbia and in resorts alike the bungalow had become a "fever" and spelled "easy housekeeping and home comforts without ostentation."[3]

In his 1913 article in *Bungalow Magazine*, Schermerhorn suggested the attractiveness of the bungalow strongly appealed to the person of moderate means, especially to apartment dwellers, who had been "educated to the rooms-on-one-floor idea, the elimination of the stair climbing act, overhead or adjoining noises, also frequently too close to ill-fitting neighbors." Such people recognized that the bungalow can be a "Godsend," a single family dwelling that still retains "all the economical

Below: The bungalow is shown here in its typical bungalow village setting. The myriad arrangements of roofs and materials make rows of bungalows visually interesting and individual. Gardens, well-maintained plantings, a garage to the rear along an alley, and even croquet on the lawn are featured. Life in the bungalow era was good. Designed by George W. Bullard of Tacoma, Washington, an area of prime bungalows, this was the Ninth Prize House in the 1927 *Delineator* competition. From *The Delineator's Prize $3,000 Houses* (New York: B. W. Dodge & Company, 1909), pages 58–59.

Opposite: With a well-thought-out bungalow plan and an attic that could be converted into a bedroom, this is a fine example of the type. The texture of the cement stucco wall finish is shown in the inset. From *Plans for Concrete Houses* (Chicago: Portland Cement Association, 1925), page 14.

All illustrations in this introduction are from the American Institute of Architects Archives.

No. 5101—The Dearborn
Robert L. Kane, Architect, Chicago, Ill.

IF you want to build a home that is as pleasant to look at as it is comfortable to live in and is yet well within average means, you can select no more suitable design than this five-room bungalow. Its economy lies not only in its first cost but in its low maintenance expense; for concrete masonry is economical to construct, and is practically free from repairs. Portland cement stucco as a wall covering is beautiful and permanent.

The house is entered from the porch through a small reception hall into the living room. This has a front bay with windows on three sides giving the effect of a sun parlor and insuring that the living room will always be bright and cheerful. Some will prefer to make one long room of the dining room and living room shown and enlarge the space marked "pantry" into one of the popular and convenient breakfast nooks.

The kitchen has good light and is arranged and equipped to lighten the housewife's work. The rear entrance is at the grade line, a desirable feature.

The full basement contains a good laundry and work shop and a boiler room and coal bin completely shut off from the rest of the rooms.

There are two good bedrooms on the left side of the house with bathroom between. The front bedroom can be entered directly from the reception hall if desired, or the connecting doorway can be omitted. The rear bedroom has a flight of stairs leading to an unfinished attic which may later be finished as an additional bedroom or a child's playroom if the owner so desires.

household labor and stepsaving features of the flat or apartment life, but in an environment close to nature where it is possible to enjoy her beauties consciously."[4]

Perhaps another reason for the proliferation of the bungalow was that "less expensive materials can be used in a bungalow than in other types without offending aesthetics. Somehow people view bungalows as rather 'rough-and-ready' and they will tolerate and even admire rough-boarded exteriors, stained or unstained, when in larger two-story dwellings the same consideration would be dubbed 'cheap.' . . . Indeed, often rough work of this sort is more desirable than the more perfect workmanship required in more pretentious structures."[5]

Despite, or perhaps because of, its popularity, the bungalow style is not easy to define. Bungalows have been built in the Western Stick style, the Prairie style, the Mission style, and a host of colonial styles from Spanish to English to Dutch. Frequently bungalows borrowed detail or form from the Swiss chalet, the Japanese temple, the Chinese pagoda, or the log cabin of the frontiersman. Marcus Whiffen coined the term "Bungaloid" to cover true bungalows as well as those structures "that do their best to look like bungalows" whatever their size or function. (Churches, apartment houses, duplexes, and other buildings were constructed to imitate the bungalow.) Whiffen notes, though, that "any attempt to classify bungalows by style categories would be beside the point, for in the minds of the designers of the best of them questions of style were secondary to considerations of planning."[6]

The importance of planning to the bungalow style was suggested in 1923 by Charles E. White, Jr., who enumerated several reasons for its popularity. "The first of these," he said, "is the convenience of having most of the rooms on one floor"; second, "the possibility it offers in the way of charmingly picturesque design"; third, the manner in which "it can be made to 'grow out of the soil' . . . as though it had always existed there, not like a new and shining blot on the horizon"; and fourth, "that it may be used with equal success on the prairie lot, at the seashore, in the hills or on mountain sites."[7] Also, White noted, "with a bungalow arrangement of rooms, longer vistas from room to room are possible and that delightfully architectural and decorative effect secured by glimpses through doorways from one room to another is increased by the bungalow plan."[8]

It was Charles Vaughn Boyd who, I think, looked at the bungalow plan with the most understanding of why it works in a dwelling. In his 1921 book he described the bungalow home as divided into three distinct units: the sleeping quarters, the family living rooms, and the service department.[9] Between these units are neutral zones. Sleeping quarters, he suggested, should open from a neutral zone, probably a hall, rather than directly from one of the family living rooms. The hall is useful not only in segregating the three areas, but in providing passage between them. The sleeping quarters acquire privacy through limited access from the rest of the house. The sleeping porch promotes privacy as well through its location away from public areas or above them.

Family living rooms include the dining room, the living room, and—an innovation of the bungalow—the den. The living room, dining room, and den might all flow into one another. One or more of the family rooms, especially the living room, might open directly onto the porch or veranda. The latter might even have an outside fireplace to expand its

PLAN No. 308

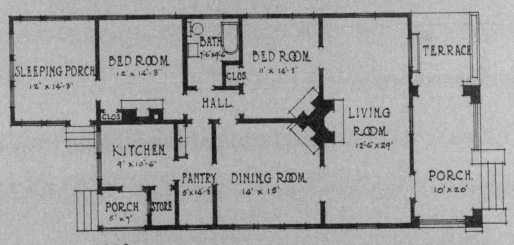

308.

FLOOR PLAN

10 FEET.

Designed for weatherboards or shingles with stucco gables and varicolored brick foundation and porch pedestals or posts, this house has everything from multiple porches to a terrace, with indoor spaces that flow out into them. Though the house features double-hung sash, the sleeping porch has casement windows. From *Homes of Distinction* (Augusta, Georgia: Scroggs and Ewing, Architects, 1922), pages 20–21.

ERNEST IRVING FREEZE, DESIGNER, LOS ANGELES, CALIFORNIA

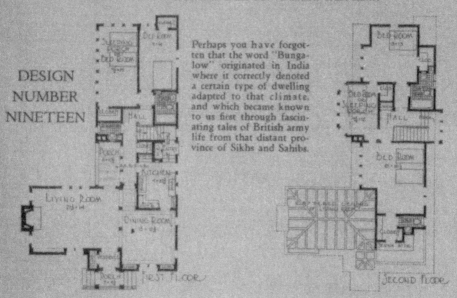

DESIGN NUMBER NINETEEN

Perhaps you have forgotten that the word "Bungalow" originated in India where it correctly denoted a certain type of dwelling adapted to that climate, and which became known to us first through fascinating tales of British army life from that distant province of Sikhs and Sahibs.

Evidently our designer was well grounded as to this origin for here he has created a bungalow true to the original pattern even in such details as thatched covering and high peaked roof lines. At the same time, he has gone the Indians one better by including a complete second floor, incidentally providing real studio atmosphere below stairs by running the living room through to the roof, which forms its decorative raftered ceiling. For you who desire a plan of some temperament, replete with good points, here is your answer—modern, well done and authentically correct.

Above: A "real California bungalow" by H. R. Shurtleff of
Virginia, this design was adaptable enough to allow two buildings of the same plan to be built beside each other without appearing to be duplicates. Different materials, color, and finish distinguish each version. Inside, room dividers—while
permanent when in place—are not load-bearing, so the interior space is fluid as well. The design confines the living quarters to one floor, though expansion into attic and basement
is easy. From H. R. Shurtleff and Mary G. Davis, *Designs
for American Homes* (New York: Architectural Corporation
Designers and Publishers, 1919), pages 12–13.

Opposite: Appearing as a single story, thatched-roof bungalow from the street, this house actually has two full stories,
with sleeping porches on both floors. The plan recognizes
living, sleeping, service, and neutral areas. This design by
Ernest Irving Freeze of Los Angeles is from plans submitted
in the *Pencil Points* Architectural Competition of 1927, spon-
sored by the Arkansas Soft Pine Bureau. From *Houses of Wood
for Lovers of Homes* (Little Rock, Arkansas: Soft Pine Bureau,
1927), page 26.

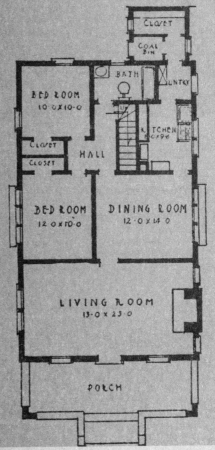

use. In William T. Comstock's introduction to this book, he wrote, "[t]o return to the veranda or, perhaps better, verandas, they should be broadly built, furnished with screens, against wind or sun, and well supplied with easy chairs, hammocks and all the paraphernalia of an outdoor summer parlor, for here will be gained the object of the bungalow, the utmost benefit of life in the open air."[10]

The service department consists primarily of the kitchen and bathroom. Neither, by the principles of bungalow planning, should open directly into the sleeping quarters. The kitchen, in locations such as the deep South or Puerto Rico, might actually be separated from the main house. Regardless of its location in the plan, however, this room is arranged so as "not to flood the other rooms with its odors, and yet to be convenient to the dining room."[11] The bathroom is most often located between sleeping and living areas of the house with its single door opening into a neutral zone.

Basically the maze of small rooms off a center hall, side hall, or corner stair hall—so common in Victorian houses of the last quarter of the nineteenth century and in other house types built between 1900 and 1930—did not appear in the bungalow. It was more flexible in plan than these houses could be, largely because of its construction. The compactness of the bungalow and its single story character normally did not require interior load-bearing walls. This meant that once the house was framed, interior walls could be added or subtracted at will and rooms could be arranged in almost endless variety.

To contribute to the open feeling of the bungalow interior, as much furniture as possible was built in and the rest was arranged in a way that would not clutter the space. In the ideal bungalow the furniture was probably Mission or Craftsman style. Every detail of the building, from the direction of the sun at a given time of day to the swing of every door and the position of each radiator, was considered. Even hardware was of prime importance and, it was suggested, "fittings for a bungalow should be as condensed as the equipment of a yacht."[12]

This attention to detail and appropriate furnishings applied to the use of color and choice of materials as well. "A Model Bungalow" was described in 1912 as being covered with cedar shakes stained a silver gray.[13] Trim was white, with green sash and dark brown lattice work. The chimney was of pressed brick, light gray in color, with weathered cobblestone. All exterior woodwork was of unsurfaced clear timber.

Inside, this model bungalow had a living room with a Rookwood tile mantel and hearth and a Mission-framed casement sash of art glass. Colors were almost always muted and organic. The bungalow was not a stark white or yellow house on a hill, nor was the interior as grim or dark as its Victorian counterpart. Interior colors were light and airy. Colors that could absorb "50 to 85 per cent of the light," such as scarlets, crimsons, browns, and deep buffs, were shunned, for light was of supreme importance in the bungalow.[14]

The value given to light on the interior and to muted colors and natural materials on the exterior reflected the bungalow style's emphasis on building a house that blended into the landscape. Charles E. White's 1923 work discussed how the bungalow was made to fit into its surroundings: "Who can forego the charm of the low, broad roof line, the little front entrance with its quaint door opening so close to the ground, the low outlines of the little building which seems to nestle so snugly

in its setting and offers so little competition with Nature as it rests modestly against the sky line, instead of rearing itself aggressively above the horizon."[15] The coziness, the snugness, beneath ceilings measurably lower than the ten- to twelve-foot heights of earlier eras, might lead one to suggest the charm of the bungalow is really in its "wombiness."

Promoting the Bungalow Aesthetic
In the United States between 1860 and 1910 the percentage of the population living in metropolitan areas had increased from less than 20 to more than 45.[16] Much of this increase was in new suburban communities, ranging from streetcar suburbs to unprecedented resort development, especially

A Craftsman interior, with exposed beam ceiling and very little decoration, is featured in the living room and dining room of this house. A library has been created in one end of the living room by bookcases serving as room dividers. From Henry H. Saylor, ed., *Inexpensive Homes of Individuality* (New York: McBride, Nast & Company, 1912), page 79.

Wide boards are laid up horizontally like clapboards on the wood frame over the underpinning of local stone

In the dining-room, as throughout the first story, the second floor joists, closely spaced, form a very decorative ceiling

THE HOME OF MR. LEICESTER K. DAVIS, LANGHORNE, PA.

Lawrence Visscher Boyd, architect

around major cities such as New York, Boston, Chicago, and Los Angeles. As one bungalow brochure put it, the population at this time was changing from "merely renters" to owners.[17] This burgeoning population of homeowners provided the readership for a rash of new house-design and decorating publications.

House Beautiful began publication in 1896, and *House and Garden* in 1901. Gustav Stickley's magazine, *The Craftsman*, was published from 1901 until 1916. All carried articles on bungalows; indeed, over the publishing span of the Stickley magazine, the bungalow received more attention than any other style of dwelling. Stickley adopted the bungalow, "a single story house whose well-ventilated rooms opened off a central airy hall, and which had a low pitched roof and a verandah on all sides," as the unofficial Craftsman house.[18]

The style had its own organ in *Bungalow Magazine*, published in Los Angeles in 1909-1910 by Henry L. Wilson. "The Bungalow Man" put out the publication more as advertising for his own bungalow business than as a true journal. Later, from 1912 to 1918, the magazine was published in Seattle by Jud Yoho, an architect whose work is included in the Comstock publication reprinted here.[19] From 1912 on, *Bungalow Magazine* was concerned with bungalow life, "not only the design and construction of the bungalow itself,

but the maintenance thereof, the surroundings, the outbuildings, gardens, lawns, etc., and . . . hints to housewives on the economical and easy management of the home."[20]

The number of other publications in the era that took up the bungalow cause was great. One of the most powerful was the *Ladies' Home Journal*, which published *Journal Bungalows* in 1921.[21] The publication noted that "the specifications are procurable for practically all of these bungalows, and we shall be glad to give you the architect's address and the price he is charging upon request." It also stated that "[h]e who deliberately builds an ugly house, condemns himself as a poor citizen, while he who builds a beautiful house proves himself a good citizen, for his personal effort contributes to the public welfare."[22]

Entire communities of bungalows were developed in the first quarter of the twentieth century, and several publicized their plans with fine publications. In 1909 "the Bungalow Colony of Neighborly Metuchen," New Jersey, with offices at 160 Broadway in New York published *Bungalow Plans* "as designed and built exclusively by the Bungalow Colony."[23] The Southern California Home Builders, operating in Los Angeles and San Diego, provided plans for new subdivisions in their area.[24]

J. L. Feibleman & Co. held a national competition in 1911 for designs of a number of "low cost California Bungalow type cottages" to be erected on its 132-acre "Florham Park Estates" near Newark, New Jersey. Two hundred fifteen designs were submitted, and the work of H. E. Warren of New York was given the first prize and a promise of construction in the development. Other competition entries may also have been executed. The program noted that the winning entry was "to contain one large living room with an open

Bungalows were not always furnished in the Craftsman or Mission style. Sometimes, as here, family furniture was used. The wide spacing of the side windows on the second level of this house and almost full dormers, front and rear, allow four possible bedrooms and a bath on the second story with room left for storage. From Saylor, *Inexpensive Homes*, page 78.

fireplace, and in addition to this four rooms, kitchen and bath. There is to be both gas and electric lighting. Building is to be of frame. Open beam ceiling in the large living room. Stucco may be used as the outside finish."[25]

During this time manufacturers of hollow tile, concrete, and other building materials also held competitions for bungalow designs. The NATCO (National Fire Proofing Co., Pittsburgh) Hollow Tile competition of 1913 produced one of the finest of the bungalow books to result from a competition. The cover shows a view from the dining room, illustrating the manner in which siting is planned to take advantage of vistas, views, or special trees, plants, or garden furniture. NATCO tile was made of terra-cotta, and it was fire resistance that these designs were meant to sell. Nevertheless, the work evidences an

Above: This house of hollow tile is shown under construction. Manufactured of burnt clay, hollow tile was usually covered with stucco. As shown here, it would have been quite normal to use brick in arches and corner bracing. The rubble or fieldstone of the chimney was a bungalow feature, which often exhibited cobblestone or combinations of stone and brick. This house is of unknown origin and location, probably about 1910.

Opposite: The concrete manufacturers matched the lumber companies in their publications for the potential homeowner, with fire resistance, durability, and sanitation touted as reasons for using concrete. This illustration, meant to show the suitability of concrete for the construction of bungalows, appeared in *The Concrete House and Its Construction* (Philadelphia: Association of American Portland Cement Manufacturers, 1912), page 190.

awareness of the special quality of the bungalow.[26]

As the number of communities and building product manufacturers flourished, so did the number of architects and manufacturers offering bungalows, many of them eager to publish catalogs to show their wares. Henry L. Wilson's *Bungalow Book* was already in its third edition by 1908. Wilson, a "designer of artistic homes," had his offices in Los Angeles and noted that "[f]rom the ' 'dobe shacks' of the early settlers to the charming homelike Bungalows of today may seem a long stretch, but it has come along as a steady process of evolution and improvement until today the California Bungalow is known and talked about the world over, and not even the glorious climate and everlasting sunshine call forth from the tourist so many comments of ad-

miration and pleasure as do these cozy homes."[27] Wilson's *Bungalow Magazine* of April 1910 carried letters from satisfied customers in Shelbina, Missouri; Mount Vernon, New York; Evanston, Illinois; Lima, Ohio; Birmingham, Alabama; Tucson, Arizona; and Bakersfield, California.

The Radford Architectural Company had published *Radford's Artistic Bungalows*, containing 208 designs, by 1908. The company, with offices in Chicago and New York, sold throughout the country: "It matters not whether it be in the city or the country, for a bungalow built after any design in this book will be an ornament anywhere."[28] The Los Angeles Investment Company, "the largest co-operative building company in the world," had published at least two editions of its *Practical Bungalows of Southern California* by

1911.[29] Ye Planry Building Company, also of Los Angeles, published the fifth edition of *Ye Planry Bungalows* in 1912.[30]

The Architectural Designing Co. of Spokane published one of the most informative bungalow books in its *Plans and Designs* of 1912. In this volume the house type was defined succinctly: "Primarily the word 'Bungalow' conveys to the mind the idea of a low, rambling, one-story dwelling, the exterior of which must be at once novel and attractive as well as simple and graceful in outline. The interior features must be designed for economy of space and utility and must typify 'home comfort' to the highest degree."[31] The company offered bungalow plans in cottage, Swiss chalet, story-and-a-half, and Mission styles. The designers recommended screened sleeping porches, a compact kitchen, and hot water or steam heat. Landscaping was also a feature they praised highly: "The surroundings and setting of the home determine in a great measure its value and merit, both from an artistic and financial point of view. Improper grounds may ruin the appearance of an otherwise artistic building, while even the simplest of landscape treatment, properly designed, cannot fail to add immensely to the value of any residence."[32]

Curtis Bros. & Co., of Clinton, Iowa, published a book of *Attractive Bungalows* in 1914, and fine houses they were. Design "C-24" even had windows in the closets.[33] Curtis did business in at least nine cities in the Midwest. De Luxe Building Co. in Los Angeles had its second edition of *The Draughtsman* bungalows out by 1912. This volume featured a bungalow of "four flats or apartments" as plan number 224. By 1914 the company was also publishing *Kozy-Homes*, a book of "inexpensive bungalows," along with *Home-Kraft-Homes* and *Plan-Kraft*.[34]

L. F. Garlinghouse of Topeka, Kansas, offered *Bungalow Homes* in 1916, asserting that "our bungalows are all well ventilated and lighted and are equipped with full cemented basements, open air sleeping porches and many built-in conveniences without which a real home is incomplete." A set of Garlinghouse plans consisted of "blue prints of four elevations, basement and all floor plans, with details of all cabinets, buffets, seats, mantels, bookcases, kitchen cupboards, etc., all drawn to scale. A sectional drawing and a roof plan, where any intricacy of construction seems to demand it," were also supplied.[35]

Though the American Institute of Architects frowned upon publications used by architects to advertise their work, many architects produced books during this era. Surely none is better than that of Raymond D. Weeks of Ridgewood, New Jersey, published in 1914.[36] Its large format showcases the wonderful drawings and fine calligraphy found throughout. Weeks noted that "it is absolutely essential that the general appearance [of the bungalow] should be of a low character, and all the exterior lines should tend to this effect." His work, entitled *The Bungalow Book*, offered bungalows in multiple styles: English thatched roof, pergola, Mission, Colonial, summer camp, and gambrel, among others. He combined materials, as did most other designers, including stucco with half timbering, brick with stucco, shingle with clapboarding, and stucco with shingle. Log, brick, and cement bungalows also appear in his work.

Bungalows, by Lindstrom and Almars, architects of Minneapolis, was published in 1915. Its cover is a guide to the colors of the style, with muted greens, grays, brown, and rose. Another edition, issued in 1922, was credited to the firm John W. Lindstrom.

A BUNGALOW OF GOOD PROPORTIONS AND ONE THAT ELIMINATES THE HEAVY FEATURES SO COMMON IN THIS TYPE OF HOUSE
THIS ECONOMICAL PLAN OFFERS A LARGE AMOUNT OF COMFORT WITHIN A LIMITED FLOOR SPACE AND FOR LITTLE MONEY

Lindstrom's designs follow all the hallmarks of the bungalow plan.[37] Leila Ross Wilburn of Atlanta published her *Southern Homes and Bungalows* in 1915, featuring examples still recognizable as types throughout the South. Her plans follow the interior arrangement as carefully as the Lindstrom ones do.[38]

The Architects' Small House Service Bureau published *Bungalows* in 1935. One of the last of the bungalow books, it contains plans for sixty houses. By that time the bureau had regional headquarters in eight cities and always admonished potential homeowners to "[e]mploy your local architect even if you should use these Bureau plans. His service, as your professional advisor and as inspector of

This simple house allows a bedroom on the second level and a full basement. One enters a small vestibule with a closet. A breakfast nook and the kitchen are on the left and the living room and rest of the house on the right. This bungalow has almost made the evolution from earlier bungalows to the ranch house and rambler that followed. From *Your Future Home*, a selection of small house plans designed by the Architects' Small House Service Bureau (St. Paul, Minnesota: Weyerhaeuser Forest Products, 1923), pages 146–147.

15

your house construction will be worth many times the fair fee he will charge."[39]

Aladdin, Sears, and Montgomery Ward, along with a number of other companies whose catalogs I have not seen, produced much more than just bungalow plans. The total house was available pre-cut and ready for assembly. Buying such a kit offered certain advantages, since owners were freed from the necessity of securing material locally and were able to determine immediately what the material costs would be. They then had only to factor in the cost of land on which to build the house and the labor required to assemble it.

In addition to their appearance in books and catalogs, bungalow designs and pre-cut kits appeared in advertisements in almost all popular magazines and daily newspapers. All in all, it would seem that the source of a good many of the bungalows still standing might be ascertained with a bit of research.

The "airplane bungalow" was a common type in the West. Having grown a two-story cabin above the fuselage, this bungalow spread its single story wings on either side. From *How to Plan Finance and Build Your Home*, published for the Southern Pine Association, New Orleans (Minneapolis: Architects' Small House Service Bureau, 1921), page 127.

Two Books on Bungalow Design

There seem to have been only two major general interest books about the bungalow. The William Phillips Comstock work reprinted here is the second edition of a work first printed in 1908 and subsequently reworked and reprinted twice.[40] The subtitle in the first edition noted that the work consists "of a large variety of designs by a number of architects, showing buildings that have been erected in all parts of the country. Many of these are intended for summer use, while other examples are of structures erected in California and the Southern States for permanent residences; also Camps, Hunters' Lodges, Log Cabins, etc., are included, suggestive for vacation use in woods and mountains."[41]

Just who William Phillips Comstock was is uncertain, but he must have had some relationship to the publishing company that issued this work, the William T. Comstock Company of New York. The company not only published architectural works but issued *Architecture and Building* weekly in the late nineteenth and early twentieth centuries. The magazine's masthead described it as "devoted to art, architecture, archaeology, engineering and decoration," and William Phillips Comstock was later its editor.[42] During the first decade of the twentieth century, the Comstock company published a series of works similar to the one reprinted here. Among them were the *Swiss Chalet Book*, by William S. B. Dana; *Two Family and Twin Houses*, by William T. Comstock; *Garages and Motor Boat Houses*, by William P. Comstock; *The Hollow Tile House*, by Frederick Squires; and *American Renaissance, a Book on the History of Domestic Colonial Architecture in America*, by Joy Wheeler Dow. It also published works on construction and decoration, including *Rumford Fireplaces and How They are Made*, by G. Curtis

Home Plan No. 6511—Contents 24,700 Cubic Feet

 The complete plans for this home are ready to use. They include working drawings, specifications and a quantity survey. They have been prepared and are owned by the Architects' Small House Service Bureau of Minnesota, Inc.—home office at 1200 Second Avenue South, Minneapolis. This Bureau has the endorsement of the American Institute of Architects. It is a group of professional architects, who, in addition to their regular practice, are able through co-operation to prepare plans and service for small homes at the lowest possible cost. See accompanying price list for cost of plans and how to secure the service.

The Aeroplane Type of House

THE aeroplane type of house is given that name from the fact of the likeness of its roof to the wings of an aeroplane. The roof has a very low pitch and is covered with canvas with prominent ridges, which increase the similarity to the aeroplane. The projection of the cornice is surmounted with a large cupola, having a remote resemblance to the cabin of the aeroplane operator. This type of house has been a great favorite in California.

The walls are covered with very wide siding. It has a brick base course and frame construction. Instead of the type of roofing as shown in the illustration ordinary shingles or tile may be used if the home builder desires, or if climatic conditions demand it. The basement is only partially excavated. It has a heater and laundry. This home will take a rather wide lot for in an attempt to get the features of a bungalow with bedrooms on the first story, it has been necessary to spread it over a rather large territory. In many ways this home combines the virtues of a bungalow with the convenience of a two-story house.

There is a sleeping porch and a bedroom on the second story which by their location at the top of the house should get every summer breeze that blows. In addition there are two bedrooms of commodious size on the first story, each one equipped with a fine closet. Each bedroom has cross ventilation.

There is a built-in linen closet on the first floor and a bathroom with good light, well arranged fixtures and convenient medicine cabinet over the lavatory. Among the numerous conveniences is a good size coat closet opening off the living room. The living room is a real one. There is a fireplace on one side of the room and opposite it a bay window provides for a setting of flowers or a comfortable seat as the owner may desire.

In an alcove separated from the living room by a cased opening, there is a space for an average size dining table. The alcove has an entrance upon a grassy terrace which may be used for an outside dining place when the weather permits. Many windows make the alcove inviting.

The kitchen has a sink underneath windows with drain board at one end and space for an ice box at the other. This space is provided with an outside icing door. There are plenty of cupboards to take care of the kitchen needs.

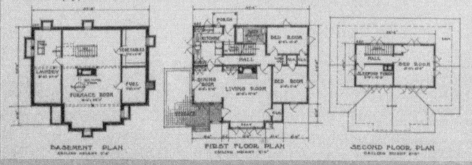

BASEMENT PLAN

FIRST FLOOR PLAN

SECOND FLOOR PLAN

Gillespie, and *Wall Papers and Wall Coverings*, by Arthur Seymour Jennings.

One notable work in this series is *The Housing Book*, by William P. Comstock, published in 1919. The work's subtitle explains its contents: "Photographic Reproductions, with Floor Plans of Workingmen's Homes. One and Two Family Houses of Frame, Brick, Stucco and Concrete Construction; also Four, Six and Nine Family Apartments. Showing Single Houses, Groups and Developments that have been built in various parts of the United States."[43] One of the more interesting chapters is "Development for Colored Workers, Truxton, Va.," by Rossell Edward Mitchell, a Norfolk architect. The work also contains developments by George Browne Post, Electus D. Litchfield, Hiss and Weeks, and, of course, "Designs for Single and Double Houses of Moderate Cost," by C. E. Schermerhorn.

Clarence Eaton Schermerhorn (1872–1925), who wrote the essay in the work reprinted here, was a native Philadelphian who studied architecture at the Spring Garden Institute and "by 1888 was in the office of senior architect Stephen Decatur Button," whom he later succeeded.[44] He established a partnership with another Spring Garden man, Henry L. Reinhold, in 1894 and afterward practiced with other partners and alone. He designed hundreds of residences and a wide variety of other building types as well as publishing his own works, with some sniping from the AIA based on its ban on advertising. He was one of the first architects in the country to use the radio, and his brochure "Services of an Architect" was read over the air on some thirty stations.[45] Schermerhorn wrote for the Comstock magazine *Architecture and Building*, and he was published in *Bungalow Magazine* and other journals.

The major competition to Comstock's *Bungalows, Camps and Mountain Houses* was Henry Saylor's *Bungalows*, published first in 1911 and reprinted in 1913, 1917, and 1926. Most of the Saylor work is taken up with discussion of bungalow construction, from plan through foundation, finish, lighting, sewage disposal, and planting. The work also spends some sixty pages defining the bungalow and developing a bungalow typology. Saylor's buildings are mostly anonymous and the architects unmentioned. This is somewhat surprising as Saylor was himself an architect and later became a pillar of the American Institute of Architects.[46]

In contrast, Comstock's book is illustrated with architect-designed buildings and architects are identified. The reader is referred to "these gentlemen where further particulars or complete drawings are desired," and Comstock provided the addresses of the architects in the book to encourage communication between them and potential clients. In his introduction he suggested "the actual preparation of the drawings is the work of the architect," but that planning "requires the careful study of the owner if he would secure from the architect a house that will be convenient to live in, and meet the personal requirements of daily life and ease in carrying on domestic work . . . . the trained architect . . . will develop your ideas, correct any deficiencies and co-ordinate the plan with the exterior design. Being conversant with costs and uses of material and labor, he will more than save his commission to the owner by economies of designing and construction."[47]

In addition to Schermerhorn's designs, those of a large number of other well-known architects appear in Comstock. Antonin

Nechodoma (1867–1928) of Puerto Rico is represented in all three editions.[48] Edition three includes an essay by O. C. Gould on "Housing in the American Tropics," which serves as a portfolio of Nechodoma's designs. Eighteen of his projects are illustrated, many with elevations and plans. Nechodoma's tropical houses include several Wrightian structures as well as early twentieth-century adaptations to Caribbean materials and conditions. He certainly designed some of the best known Caribbean residences of this century. The Gould essay—"All designs should give due regard to climate, sun, rain, and pests of various sorts"—covers insulation, earthquake protection, the importance of complete screening, and a warning against lead, especially when cisterns were used to trap rainwater from the roof for household use.

Guy King of Philadelphia, whose works were published in *American Architect and Building News*, is another of the architects included.[49] David Knickerbacker Boyd (Philadelphia)[50]; A. W. Cobb (Springfield, Massachusetts)[51]; Davis, McGrath and Shepard (New York)[52]; and John Calvin Stevens (Portland, Maine)[53] also produced work that frequently appeared in that publication. Trost & Trost (El Paso)[54] and Robert H. Orr (Los Angeles)[55] appeared frequently in *American Architect*. The entire July 1911 issue of *Southern Architectural Review* was devoted to the work of C. W. Bulger (Dallas),[56] while F. G. Lippert's (New York) work appeared in the *Deutsche bauzeitung*.[57] The men included in the Comstock book—there are no designs by women—were all highly regarded professionals. The book thus serves as a record of some of the best work the architecture profession carried out in the bungalow style.

Influence of the Bungalow

In his discussion of the style, Marcus Whiffen notes that it was the bungalow "as much as any other kind of house that led to the general adoption of the 'living room' and the 'outdoor-indoor' living space."[58] After the bungalow was dead, these ideas survived in the Usonian houses of Frank Lloyd Wright and in the best of the contemporary houses of the immediate post–World War II era. They are alive again today in open plans as well as in plans that site the house more carefully in its setting, preserve trees and natural vegetation, and attempt to integrate the building into its natural environment with as little disruption as possible. That studies are now being produced on the bungalow and that it has again become popular as a residence should come as no surprise.

Tony P. Wrenn, AIA Archivist

Acknowledgments

The work being reprinted here is from the Rare Books and Special Collections of the American Institute of Architects Library in Washington, D.C. All material consulted in the introduction is also either a part of that collection or of the collections of the Library of Congress in Washington. The assistance of Melissa Houghton is gratefully acknowledged. Lee Stallsworth was the copy photographer for the illustrations used in the introduction. Prints and negatives of these are in the AIA Archives Collection. Pamela Blumgart copyedited the introduction, and Marilyn Worseldine designed the cover and other new material.

Endnotes

Readers interested in studying early twentieth-century works on the bungalow may find it useful first to look at current literature on the history and lure of the bungalow. Clay Lancaster's *The American Bungalow, 1880–1930* (New York: Abbeville Press, 1985) remains the best single work, and most libraries should have it. *The California Bungalow,* by Robert Winter (California Architecture and Architects Series, no. 1; Los Angeles: Hennessey & Ingalls, 1980), is also worth taking a look at, as is Anthony D. King's *The Bungalow: The Production of a Global Culture* (London: Routledge and Kegan Paul, 1984). King's Chapter 4, "North America 1880-1980," is particularly readable and informative. Dover has reprinted *Craftsman Homes* and *More Craftsman Homes,* as well as *Craftsman Bungalows* (New York: Dover Publications, 1988), which includes thirty-six articles from *The Craftsman* magazine between December 1903 and August 1916. This reprint of the 1915 Comstock/Schermerhorn *Bungalows, Camps and Mountain Houses* should also find ready use by the bungalow dweller, owner, or aficionado. Out of print since 1924, it provides one of the best looks at architect-designed bungalows, with plans and elevations, combined with a most readable text that enlivens and illuminates the bungalow idea.

1. R. A. Briggs, *Bungalows and Country Residences* (London: B. T. Batsfod, 1901), p. v.

2. C. E. Schermerhorn, "Plan Studies of Bungalows," *Bungalow Magazine* 2 (October 1913), p. 48.

3. Schermerhorn, p. 46.

4. Schermerhorn, p. 46.

5. Charles E. White, Jr., *The Bungalow Book* (New York: MacMillan, 1923), p. 8.

6. Marcus Whiffen, *American Architecture since 1780: A Guide to the Styles* (Cambridge: The MIT Press, 1981), pp. 217, 221.

7. White, p. 7.

8. White, p. 9.

9. Charles Vaughn Boyd, *The Little Book of Bungalows and Cottages* (New York: Woman's Home Companion, 1921), p. 8.

10. William P. Comstock, *Bungalows, Camps and Mountain Houses* (New York: The William T. Comstock Co., 1915), p. 13.

11. Comstock, *Bungalows,* p. 13.

12. Comstock, *Bungalows,* p. 21.

13. Jud Yoho, "A Model Bungalow," *Bungalow Magazine* 1 (August 1912), pp. 30–32.

14. Comstock, *Bungalows,* p. 21.

15. White, p. 6.

16. Anthony D. King, *The Bungalow: The Production of a Global Culture* (London: Routledge and Kegan Paul, 1984), p. 138.

17. *Southern California Bungalow Plans* (Los Angeles: Southern California Home Builders, 1913), inside front cover.

18. Gustav Stickley, *Craftsman Bungalows*, Introduction by Alan Weissman (New York: Dover Publications, 1988), p. vi.

19. Yoho, the "Bungalow Craftsman" of Seattle, had also published the *Craftsman Bungalow Co.* book by 1913. It had a fine cover in gray, green, and gold. A new edition of that book was out by 1916, and by 1921 he had published *Colonial Homes*, featuring the "New Colonial Bungalow."

20. The "Housewife's Corner" did not survive until 1918, but was a casualty of a 1913 reader survey in which 62 percent of the respondents suggested it be eliminated. It is possible the column did not sufficiently mirror the simplicity of bungalow life. When asked in 1912 to suggest a "simple menu for Christmas dinner" in a bungalow, the columnist, Mrs. M. E. Stacy, recommended "Raw oysters served with sliced lemon, turtle soup, baked fresh fish; roast turkey, garnished with fried oysters, dressing; mashed potatoes; lima beans; pickled beets; chicken salad; celery; cranberry sauce; Christmas plum pudding with rice sauce; mince pie; coffee; fruit and nuts." Hardly simple, cozy, or unostentatious.

21. The book included designs by Gertrude A. Luckey and Gertrude Luckey Waldron, giving a look at the practice of this woman architect before and after her marriage.

22. *Journal Bungalows* (Philadelphia: The Ladies Home Journal, 1921), p. 3.

23. *Bungalow Plans* (New York: The Bungalow Colony of Neighborly Metuchen, 1909).

24. *Southern California Bungalow Plans*, title page.

25. AIA Archives, RG 802, SR 2, Box 3, Folder 19.

26. National Fire Proofing Company, *The NATCO Bungalow* (Boston: Rogers & Manson Co., 1913), p. 3: "Generally speaking [a home] is, or is not, a bungalow according to the feeling—expression—in the design."

27. Henry L. Wilson, *The Bungalow Book* (Los Angeles: Henry L. Wilson, 1908), p. 4. This work has a wonderful cover in browns and greens. On the title page is a cut of "The House Beautiful" showing a bungalow with the sign "Wilson Bungalows."

28. *Radford's Artistic Bungalow* (Chicago: The Radford Architectural Co., 1908), p. 3. Their offices are listed at 185 East Jackson Boulevard in Chicago and 261 Broadway in New York.

29. *Practical Bungalows of Southern California* (Los Angeles: Los Angeles Investment Company, 1911). At 333-335-337 South Hill Street, they called themselves "The largest co-operative building company in the world."

30. *Ye Planry Bungalows* (Los Angeles: Ye Planry Building Company, Inc., 1912). Offices were at 536 Title Insurance Building.

31. *Plans and Designs of Bungalows, Modern Homes, Churches, Schools, etc.* (Spokane, Washington: Architectural Designing Co., 1912), unnumbered pages. Offices were in the Realty Building.

32. *Bungalows, Modern Homes, Churches, Schools.*

33. *Attractive Bungalows* (Clinton, Iowa: Curtis Bros. & Co., 1914). Other Curtis Co. offices were in Warsaw, Wisconsin; Detroit, Michigan; Pittsburgh, Pennsylvania; Minneapolis, Minnesota; Lincoln, Nebraska; Sioux City, Iowa; Oklahoma City, Oklahoma; and Chicago, Illinois.

34. *The Draughtsman* (Los Angeles: DeLuxe Building Co., 1912) and *Kozy Homes* (Los Angeles: DeLuxe Building Co., 1914). Their offices were at 521-523 Union League Building, and they advertised "Inexpensive Bungalows."

35. *Bungalow Homes* (Topeka: L. F. Garlinghouse, 1915). Their offices were in Suite 418, Oxford Building. This work had gone through three editions by 1922. That edition lists J. Ralph Brunt as architect, E. M. Jones as draftsman, and Iva G. Lieurance as designer.

36. Weeks's title page calls the work "a collection of perspective drawings of modern bungalows" and notes it was "designed and published by Raymond D. Weeks, Architect, Osmur Building, Ridgewood, New Jersey." It is a large-scale, extremely handsome volume.

37. Lindstrom and Almars, *Bungalows* (Minneapolis: Lindstrom and Almars, 1915). The cover of this edition is a study in bungalow colors, with muted greens, grays, brown, and rose. It shows a bungalow nestled in a natural setting with a woman and child leaving the house.

38. Leila Ross Wilburn, *Southern Homes and Bungalows* (Atlanta: Leila Ross Wilburn, circa 1915). With offices at 305 Peters Building, Wilburn labels her work "a collection of choice designs." The work shows bungalows actually built, and the variety, design, and plans are excellent examples of the style.

39. *Bungalows* (Minneapolis: The Architects Small House Service Bureau, 1935), p. 64. Contains "sixty . . . bungalows and story and a half homes designed by architects of national prominence," none of whom are identified.

40. William P. Comstock, *Bungalows, Camps and Mountain Houses* (New York: William T. Comstock Co.). The first edition was published in 1908, the second in 1915, and the third in 1924. Presumably the author, William P., was related to the publisher, William T.

41. Comstock, *Bungalows* (1908), title page. No biographical data on William Phillips Comstock were located, though he clearly was the developer of this volume.

42. *Architecture and Building* 20 (January-June 1894).

43. William P. Comstock, *The Housing Book* (New York: William T. Comstock Co., 1919).

44. See Sandra L. Tatman and Roger W. Moss, *Biographical Dictionary of Philadelphia Architects, 1700-1930* (Boston:

G. K. Hall & Co., 1985), pp. 696–702.

   45. Henry F. Withey and Elsie Rathburn Withey, *Biographical Dictionary of American Architects Deceased* (Los Angeles: Hennessey & Ingalls Inc., 1970), p. 539.

   46. See *Who Was Who in America*, vol. 4 (Chicago: Marquis–Who's Who, Inc., 1968) p. 831. Saylor edited *Architectural Review* (1904–1906); *American Architect* (1909); *House and Garden* (1909–1911); his own journal, *Architect's World* (1938); *Journal of the American Institute of Architects* (1944–1957), and was an associate editor at *Architectural Forum* (1938–1941). He compiled a popular architectural dictionary (1952) and wrote *The AIA's First 100 Years* (Washington: The American Institute of Architects, 1957).

   47. Comstock, *Bungalows*, pp. 12, 16.

   48. No biography of Nechodoma has been located though he deserves thorough study. See Withey and Withey, p. 438.

   49. See *American Architect and Building News* 75 (January 25, 1902), p. 31, plate 1361, and AIA Archives, RG 803, Box 3, Volume 1, p. 130.

   50. See Tatman and Moss, pp. 89–92. The *Avery Index* lists multiple entries for Boyd in *American Architect and Building News*, *American Architect*, and *Architectural Record*. Boyd papers in the AIA Archives are in RG 801, SR 5.2.

   51. See *American Architect and Building News* 13 (March 17, 1883), p. 127, plate 377, and 26 (December 14, 1889), pp. 282–283.

   52. See *American Architect and Building News* 90 (July 14, 1906), p. 16, plate 1594. AABN has multiple entries on the work of Davis, McGrath and Kiessling.

   53. At least five entries between 1885 and 1903 appear in *American Architect and Building News*. His obituary appears in *Architectural Record* 72 (April 1940), p. 112, supplement.

   54. *American Architect* 131 (January 20, 1927); 137 (May 1930); and 143 (November 1933). See also Withey and Withey, p. 606.

   55. *American Architect* 144 (August 21, 1916). Multiple articles on Orr's work also appeared in *Architect and Engineer of California* and *Architectural Forum*. See also AIA Archives, RG 803, Box 140, Folder 13.

   56. See also AIA Archives, RG 803, Box 279, Folder 53.

   57. Several entries in *Deutsche bauzeitung* (vol. 27) during 1893.

   58. Whiffen, p. 221.

Opposite:
Cover design for the 1915 edition
of *Bungalows, Camps and Mountain Houses*

23

PREFACE TO THE 1915 EDITION

IN this new edition a considerable number of illustrations have been added and only a small portion of those which appeared in the first edition are retained. The total number of designs is much increased. In choosing designs full consideration was given to good planning, and good points in a plan were considered even more important than an attractive exterior illustration in determining the selection. It is hoped that the variety presented is such that the requirements of most any one contemplating the construction of a bungalow may be satisfied. The presentation of the subject matter has been improved and the designs grouped into three classes.

The contribution by Mr. Schermerhorn is a most valuable one and greatly increases the worth of the work. The descriptions of the designs are much more abbreviated than those which appeared in the first edition and these descriptions are placed near the illustrations to which they refer.

As in the first edition, a list of contributors with their addresses is given and the architect's name is generally mentioned in connection with each design.

The introduction to the first edition, which was written by William T. Comstock, who compiled that edition, is reprinted in full.

WILLIAM PHILLIPS COMSTOCK.

List of Contributors

Aimar, L. Jerome...Navesink, N. J.

Barnes, A. S.. ....Los Angeles, Cal.

Boyd, D. Knickerbacker, F. A. I. A...N.E. Cor. 15th & Walnut Sts., Philadelphia, Pa.

Bulger, C. W. & Son...............................Pretorian bldg., Dallas, Texas.

Cobb, Albert Winslow.........................509 Stearn bldg., Springfield, Mass.

Davis, McGrath & Shepard.........................Fuller bldg., New York, N. Y.

Deitrich, E. G. W.............................118 East 28th St., New York, N. Y.

Dodds, Everett S...................................613 Paxton block, Omaha, Neb.

Green, I. H...Greeley Avenue, Sayville, N. Y.

Hawkins, J. H. W...................................Realty bldg., Jacksonville, Fla.

King, Guy.......................................1513 Walnut St., Philadelphia, Pa.

Koeth, L. A. H...............................202 Orange St., Wilmington, N. C.

La Pointe & Sumner....................989 Southern Boulevard, New York, N. Y.

Lent, Frank T..Leominster, Mass.

Lippert, Frank G...............................132 Nassau St., New York, N. Y.

Manning, Harry James (formerly Wagner & Manning)..Majestic bldg., Denver, Col.

Nechodoma, Antonin..........Royal Bank of Canada bldg., San Juan, Porto Rico.

Orr, Robert H.................. 13th floor, I. N. Van Nuys bldg., Los Angeles, Cal.

Petersen, Jens C............................State Bank bldg., Traverse City, Mich.

Reid, Francis W...............................648 Call bldg., San Francisco, Cal.

Schermerhorn, C. E., A. A. I. A..................430 Walnut St., Philadelphia, Pa.

Seymour & Schonewald.................Grand Central Terminal, New York, N. Y.

Starrett, F. M...Forest Grove, Oregon.

Stevens, John Calvin..............................187 Middle St., Portland, Me.

Stroop, D. V................................424 James bldg., Chattanooga, Tenn.

Titus, Lloyd....................................430 Walnut St., Philadelphia, Pa.

Trost & Trost...................................Mills bldg., El Paso, Texas.

Webster, Geo. J..Pasadena, Cal.

Wieger, T. Robt..Denver, Colo.

Wolf, Frank D. (formerly Wolf & McKenzie)..67 W. Santa Clara St., San Jose, Cal.

Woodruffe, Arnott............................601 Tacoma bldg., Tacoma, Wash.

Yoho, Jud...................................4718 Second Ave., N.E., Seattle, Wash.

A·SMALL·BRICK·HOUSE·OF·BUNGALOW·TYPE·
·COST·$5,000·

·LA·POINTE·&·SUMNER·
·ARCHITECTS·

The Bungalow

THE word bungalow is an Anglo-Indian term, and was originally applied to a class of houses, usually of one story, occupied by Europeans in India. While the term, as a rule, refers to a house having rooms only on the ground floor, yet frequently a second story is added, containing a few rooms.

In India there are many large and elaborate houses of this class. The name is also applied to houses of a public character, established by the government for the convenience of the traveler, similar to the caravanserai of the natives. There are also military bungalows used as barracks for soldiers. These buildings are universally light-built structures intended for a warm climate or for summer use, and a special feature is the extension of the roof so as to form verandas, surrounding the living rooms of the house.

Their special adaptation to warm weather probably led to their adoption in England, by returning East Indians, for summer houses and from there the idea has traveled across the sea to us.

In this country the bungalow has been adopted both as a transient summer residence, and in California and many of the Southern States as an all-the-year-round dwelling. While some of these buildings are very simple and of low cost, others are elaborate and expensive.

The main idea of the bungalow, however, is a warm-weather house where the temperature is such as to make living in the open desirable, and the veranda follows as a logical consequence, as it is made practically the living apartment in fair weather and is usually fitted out as such.

The selection of site in these houses is quite as important, no matter how simple and cheap the structure, as in the case of a permanent dwelling.

Those building them for permanent occupation will naturally use the same caution as in other residences, but persons who are putting up summer dwellings are too apt to give these matters less consideration than is their due.

Good pure water, whether from spring, well or flowing pipe, is an essential, and without it the brief summer holiday is likely to be had at the risk of health if not life itself.

The disposal of household waste and the sanitary arrangements demand the same care as in the permanent house. This does not necessarily mean large expense, but it does mean careful attention. While it is not the purpose of this book to enter very fully into this subject of sanitation, yet it may be remarked that there are a number of good books on the subject which furnish information of a very practical character, and merit careful perusal on the part of persons intending to establish a summer home in the woods, mountains or on the lakes or seashore.

Disregard of these matters has made many resorts of great natural advantage veritable pest holes.

Often the lake or stream which has been the most attractive feature of a site has been rendered noxious by the drainage from the dwellings on its shore. Whereas, this matter, if properly considered at the start, could have been so handled as to maintain the original purity of the adjacent waters. Of late years sanitarians have given so much study to these matters that they are able to provide methods of draining safely and unobtrusively at comparatively moderate cost. The expense of treating sewage will necessarily depend largely on the magnitude of the operations, whether it be for a single dwelling or a group of dwellings. If the scheme is a large one and on new grounds, it will be well to call in a sanitary engineer.

The selection of site also has to do with the outlook, the possible arrangement of grounds, and there also the professional advice of the architect and landscape gardener will be found of great value.

While the actual preparation of the drawings is the work of the architect, yet the subject of planning requires the careful study of the owner if he would secure from the architect a house that will be convenient to live in, and meet the personal requirements of daily life and ease in carrying on domestic work. Many things that are needful in the city house or winter homes would be found unnecessary and often cumbersome in the summer bungalow. The dweller in these houses aims at least for the time to approach the simple life, and this should be recognized in the arrangement and the furnishing of such houses.

As will be seen by glancing over the accompanying plans, they vary from the simple cabin of two and three rooms to those of large dimensions suitable for large families and liberal entertainment.

The large and commodious living room with its airy windows is common to all. This room in some of those of smaller dimensions answers for the dining room as well.

The kitchen is in some cases separated from the main house and almost invariably is so arranged as not to flood the other rooms with its odors, and yet to be convenient to the dining room.

The planning should always recognize a common center, about which the other rooms cluster so as to make all convenient of access. It will not do to plan your floor, as though you had simply grouped the rooms like a lot of boxes set together, and yet the plan must not be too much scattered. Regard must also be had to good ventilation and lighting. The ventilation, as in any case, is especially important for the bedrooms.

It must not be forgotten that at the seashore or lake and in the mountain and woods there are frequently stormy days and cold evenings even in the midst of summer. It is therefore necessary to provide means of heating not only for the main living room, but also for the principal bedrooms.

In some of the designs it will be seen that one large room occupies the whole of the second story. This will be found often convenient as a dormitory when a sudden influx of visitors calls for extra sleeping accommodations.

The requirements for bathrooms and many of the other appointments of the house are much the same as in the ordinary country house.

To return to the veranda or, perhaps better, verandas, they should be broadly built, furnished with screens, against wind or sun, and well supplied with easy chairs, hammocks and all the paraphernalia of an outdoor summer parlor, for here will be gained the object of the bungalow, the utmost benefit of life in the open air.

William T. Comstock.

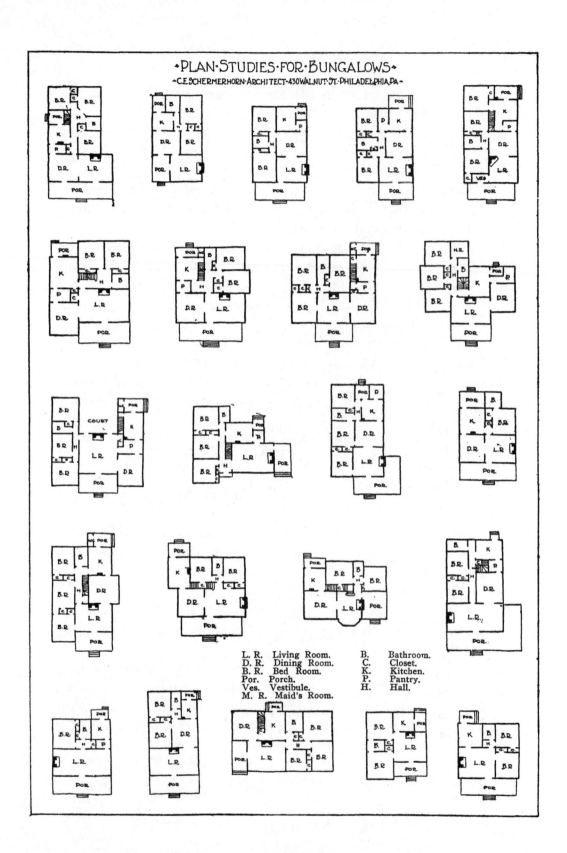

PLAN·STUDIES·FOR·BUNGALOWS

~C.E.SCHERMERHORN·ARCHITECT·430 WALNUT·ST·PHILADELPHIA.PA~

L. R.	Living Room.	B.	Bathroom.
D. R.	Dining Room.	C.	Closet.
B. R.	Bed Room.	K.	Kitchen.
Por.	Porch.	P.	Pantry.
Ves.	Vestibule.	H.	Hall.
M. R.	Maid's Room.		

Planning the Bungalow

By C. E. Schermerhorn, A. A. I. A.

THE advantage of bungalow building is that one can choose a site in sympathy with one's nature and build as one pleases, with freedom as to design and no limit set upon outlay. The bungalow need not be refused admittance to any community on the score of cost, for it can be built as cheaply or expensively as may be desired. Choose the site carefully; consider healthfulness, location, command of view, shade, soil, facilities for drainage and for water supply. Avoid a treeless site or one located considerably below the general street level, even if of low cost, as the amount of work necessary to improve and fit such a lot may bring its cost up higher than some more expensive location without these defects. In viewing a lot, calculate possible costs of grading, lawn, drives and walks.

In working out the plans for a bungalow the first task is to study the site so as to have the principal rooms face the sunshine or a desirable view; and also to consider the effects of irregularities of level on the plan. The bungalow is just as adaptable to any climate as any other style of house, and can be made just as warm and comfortable at no greater cost.

The plan is the fundamental thing that determines the success or non-success of any building; it is the most important element regardless of size; and many conveniences that should be in every modern bungalow are often missing for want of plan study. The bungalow "plan studies" plate shown, includes many arrangements of bungalow plan and is intended to assist the bungalow builder in reasoning out and determining the required number and grouping of the rooms. Time should be taken to think the plan out and get proper economy of space. Only when the plan is satisfactorily and definitely settled is the prospective bungalow-builder in a position to proceed intelligently and avoid expensive mistakes and omissions which can seldom be rectified in a satisfactory manner. There have never yet been devised or laid down any hard-

PLANNING THE BUNGALOW

and-fast rules to govern the planning of the bungalow. Personal habits and ideas are all important factors, and that which might be inadequate for one might be perfectly satisfactory to another. The plan arrangement should be convenient for every day use. All who use the bungalow should find what they want without too many steps, trouble or conflict. Get directness with each room in natural relation to the other, with free lines of travel to the entrances. The living rooms should be preferably on the eastern side, where they receive the first sunlight in the morning and are in shade in the afternoon. Fashion should not be preferred to fitness and the plan selected should be one that will outlive fads and fashions.

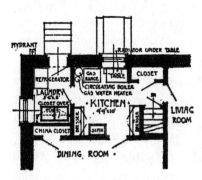

A bungalow kitchen planned for gas range only. A coal range could be used instead.

Take a piece of paper and along the lines suggested, fit to your needs and requirements one of the plans herein presented. Keep the plan simple. The more angles the more costly, as the plan adopted must naturally express itself in the exterior. The best plan to adopt is the one which shows no effort to make itself interesting except through fitness of purpose, directness, balance, adaptability, utility, privacy for family, facilities for entertainment, personal safety and convenience of the inhabitants. Study to acquire a modern, efficient, and "liveable" plan in accord with available materials of construction which are to be used judiciously. It is important to have the bungalow easy to maintain and keep in repair. But upon these points professional advice is essential.

The trained architect will develop your ideas, correct any deficiencies and co-ordinate the plan with the exterior design. Being conversant with costs and uses of materials and labor, he will more than save his commission to the owner by economies of designing and construction. He will prepare proper specifications and the detail scale drawings, obtain the builder's bids for construction and superintend the work, securing for the owner a complete building in accordance with his needs.

For a bungalow most any building material or type of construction is applicable; frame enclosed either with shingle or clapboard; stone, rough or dressed; face brick; texture tile; concrete; stucco applied to frame, brick, stone or hollow tile construction; also shakes, rustic boards, slabs and logs. Deliberate carefully over the material to be selected, keeping in mind that the bungalow should fit the site and surroundings. The difference between a structure that evokes exclamations of approval from those who pass, and one which is never noticed, is often but a well proportioned detail here or an inexpensive feature there—the difference between art and clumsiness. Modern methods of construction give preference to those materials which can be used immediately upon delivery, and which possess the necessary features of economy, quality and adaptation to good workmanship and results. The materials most easily obtained in the local market are usually the most economical.

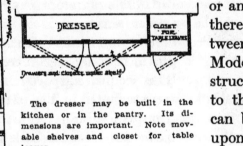

The dresser may be built in the kitchen or in the pantry. Its dimensions are important. Note movable shelves and closet for table leaves.

Our sense of sight is continuously either delighted or offended by pleasing combinations or by those that quarrel or clash, therefore try for architectural comeliness, proportion and solidity. A bungalow home is deserving of the same attention and care as a more imposing or important structure. Fashions in architecture we shall have, as we have fashions in attire, but they are ephemeral and convenience in planning should not be sacrificed to outer form. The size of doors and windows should not be subordinated to anything but actual requirements and convenience, but spacing of windows and door openings, breaks, groupings, etc., can be studiously adjusted to effect a proper exterior composition.

The bungalow porch should be readily accessible from the main hall or artery of the house and should have proper exposure and protection against sun, drafts or the elements. The width of

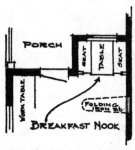

In the bungalow kitchen a Pullman alcove or breakfast nook is convenient, so also a folding ironing board.

the porch should be generous, so as to provide ample space for passage about chairs and other furniture. The porch may adjoin or connect with a floored terrace which may be covered with a pergola or left uncovered. Removable sash provided to enclose the porch in winter make it useful as a sun parlor and in colder climates radiator connections are also recommended. The radiators may be removed for the summer season and the glazed sash replaced with wire screens. Open fireplaces are often provided on large porches which are used almost as living rooms. The need of supports for swinging seats and hammocks should be anticipated. The service porch should be enclosed with a wood lattice or insect wire for summer use and it is frequently provided with movable sash for winter use in cold climates.

It is often desirable to provide a permanent sleeping porch in connection with one or more bedrooms, for sleeping in the open air is both attractive and beneficial. A permanent sleeping porch, to be convenient, should have an entrance from a bedroom, and when possible from a hall; also proper exposure and protection from varying weather conditions. The interior finish and floors should be of such a character as to be the least injured or defaced by dampness or exposure to the sun's direct rays. Complete screening, together with casement or removable sash is advised. Dining or breakfast porches are often an adjunct of the bungalow. Opening from the dining room in a secluded location, they may be enclosed with French windows.

Flower boxes at windows and on porches add so greatly to

the artistic and homelike effect of the bungalow, both indoors and out, that it is always a matter of surprise that they are not more universally employed. There is no house so small and simple in its architecture as not to be made attractive by boxes of bright flowers blooming beneath the windows and along the railing of the porches; the open window framing a mass of bright blossoms, with a back ground of sky and trees has all the value of a beautiful picture and brings the "out-of-doors" with its bloom and perfume into the shadowy rooms, brightening and freshening them as nothing else can do. The boxes should be tightly jointed and leaded to prevent leaking of water, with one small hole in one corner close to the bottom to be closed with a wood plug which may be withdrawn when necessary. The best filling is decomposed sod or soil prepared of one part ordinary loam, one part leaf mold or turfy matter mixed together with enough sharp sand to make the whole so friable that it will fall apart readily after squeezing it in the hand.

In the interior study the swing of every door, position of each register or radiator, light outlet and automatic lighting switch, bell, telephone, etc., and in each room on the plans determine and draw in the location of the furniture. Plain inside doors and trim look well and are less expensive. Interior paneling and beamed ceiling effects should be of the utmost simplicity, and all interior trim dainty and graceful. Consider the use of mirrors, skilfully employed they can do wonders towards creating an impression of space and light. Do not overlook the fact that no small detail can lend more distinction to a bungalow than its hardware, if well executed.

Think of sun windows and alcoves when planning, as they provide comfortable resting places and emergency positions for plants or ferns used for interior embellishment. Frequently window seats can be artistically incorporated in such locations. Casement windows, affording full openings, are only desirable when the sashes are designed to open out and the required insect screens arranged to open inwardly.

To seat oneself before a glowing fireplace after a damp or

chilly day is to enjoy a treat indeed. Artistic fireplaces can be created with tile, brick, stone, either dressed or rough, or cobblestones; design them in keeping with the interior. Provide a flue of adequate size, terra cotta lined and of sufficient height. There are rules which should be followed for properly building fireplaces and flues, and this information can be obtained from several good books on heating. Often the fireplace is the only means of heat in a bungalow and it is important to have it centrally located and

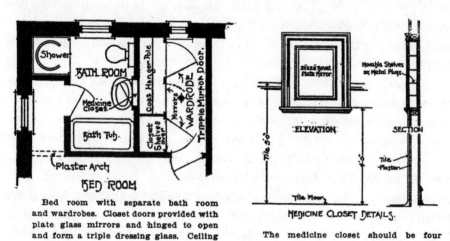

Bed room with separate bath room and wardrobes. Closet doors provided with plate glass mirrors and hinged to open and form a triple dressing glass. Ceiling light above.

The medicine closet should be four feet from floor and built into the wall.

well built, so as to drive the dampness out of the house and distribute the heat.

As most of the household tasks have to be performed in the kitchen, every step saved in that part of the home saves untold energy through a lifetime of occupation in domestic duties. Plan carefully the location of the range, sink, refrigerator, larder, dresser, table and chairs, in their relation to the doors and windows, realizing that a good outdoor view is a great asset, and the open window affording fresh air to inhale and good light is a wonderful stimulant to the worker. Well placed conveniences in the kitchen consist of such things as a properly designed kitchen dresser, ironing-board hinged and folded into a wall closet and a linen dryer sliding into a ventilated drying closet, a folding wall table and other accessories. For ventilation, which is always important in the kitchen, a swinging transom may be inserted over the kitchen door. A composition floor with sanitary base (all corners rounded) is advantageous, and a small trap in the kitchen floor connecting with the house drain is a great convenience in cleaning up. The small breakfast alcove off the kitchen is a good thing to plan for; if necessary, this may be curtained or screened off from the rest of the room. There should be a window at the end of the alcove with two benches built in at either side of a small center table.

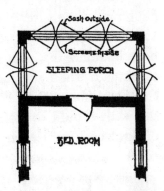

Sleeping porch opening from bed room. Provided with outside casement sash and inside screens.

The absorption of artificial light by the injudicious selection of wall coverings should be considered as a factor in the higher cost of living, and few people are aware how much light is thus wasted or thrown away. Confine interior decorations to the use of light and airy shades, avoiding scarlets, crimsons, browns and deep buffs which will absorb from 50 to 85 per cent of light. The type of artificial lighting to be installed should be carefully considered, whether lamps, gas, acetelyne or electricity, and appropriate locations should be determined for the fixtures selected. This subject is receiving much attention now and there are good new books on the subject.

Fittings for a bungalow should be as condensed as the equipment of a yacht. There are many devices and features that may be employed: the built-in buffet, crystal and china closets for the dining room, bookcases, medicine closets, folding washstands, etc. Other space savers consist of disappearing beds, double purpose revolving furniture, collapsing rod clothes-hangers for closets, and shoe racks. Full length triple mirrors can be made by hanging two mirrored doors, left and right, each side of a centre mirrored panel or door.

Good heating results depend just as much on the way the

structure is built as on the heating outfit, since both comfort and economy depend on how much warmth artificially created by the heating apparatus is kept inside. The type of heating should be determined when planning.

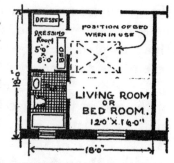

In the selection of carpets or rugs, hangings, furniture, wall coverings, pictures and ornaments for the bungalow, bear in mind that the more intimate the apartment, the more individual should be the furnishing. The choice of colors for the walls should be settled by the amount of light each particular room receives. A room that has a warm, bright, sunny expo-

Living room or bed room combination.

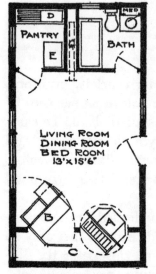

Convertible furniture economizes space. A, bed and buffet, B, bookcase and bureau. C, closet. D, sink. E, gas range. G, clothes dryer.

sure, needs a different wall color than a room so located that the only light is a cold north light or the early morning sunshine. North rooms should be treated with warm rich tones; south rooms with cool colors and dull tints. The more simple the wall decorations and draperies, the less easily you will tire of them; therefore, if you cannot afford to redecorate your house more often than is necessary, beware of striking designs, no matter how beautiful or artistic they may be in themselves. The furnishing of a bungalow should be undertaken with enthusiasm and pursued with leisure. It provides an opportunity for individual treatment and the chief rule to be observed is to secure harmony, avoid eccentricities and ignore fads.

Avoid mixed, promiscuous or haphazard furnishings as the most dangerous of household expedients and consider that a house must be lived in to realize the fullest measure of success.

BUNGALOWS

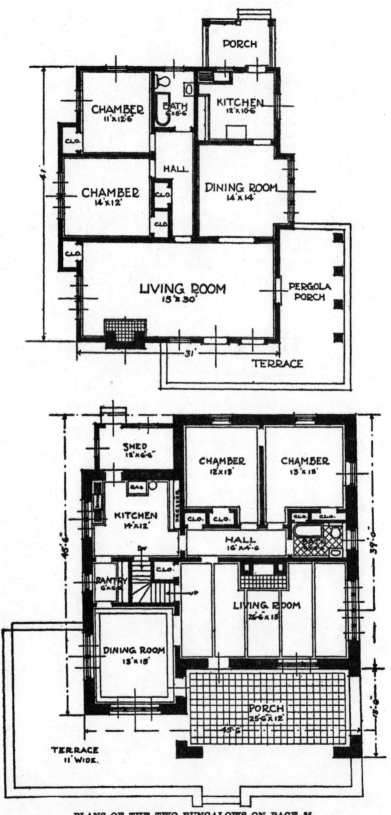

PORCH

CHAMBER
11'x12'6"

BATH
6'x6'6"

KITCHEN
12'x10'6"

HALL

CHAMBER
14'x12'

CLO.

DINING ROOM
14'x14'

CLO.

CLO.

CLO.

LIVING ROOM
15'x30'

PERGOLA
PORCH

31'

TERRACE

SHED
12'x6'6"

CHAMBER
12'x15'

CHAMBER
13'x15'

KITCHEN
14'x12'

CLO.

CLO.

CLO.

CLO.

HALL
16'x4'6"

PANTRY
6'x6'6"

CLO.

LIVING ROOM
26'6"x15'

DINING ROOM
13'x15'

PORCH
25'6"x12'

45'6"

TERRACE
11' WIDE.

PLANS OF THE TWO BUNGALOWS ON PAGE 25.

42

WELL APPOINTED AND PICTURESQUE BUNGALOW.

C. E. Schermerhorn, Architect.

AN IDEAL BUNGALOW.

(Described on page 27)

D. Knickerbacker Boyd, Architect.

BUNGALOW AT ROBBINS POINT, GRINDSTONE ISLAND, ST. LAWRENCE RIVER, N. Y.

(Described on page 27)

The picturesque is strongly expressed in the first bungalow plan shown. The chief problem of how to use a limited space to the greatest advantage has been well met in this direct and liveable plan. The utter simplicity of the exterior needs no description. A fireplace on the outside might be to the point, so that the family on chilly evenings could group around same in true camp style.

It is rare to find a plan and exterior in such thorough accord as that shown in the plan and sketch of the next bungalow. The body of the house is of grey stone laid upon flat beds in long lengths with pebble dashed gables and a green glazed tile roof; the trimmings for frames, cornices, etc., being ivory white with dark green for sashes. The front terrace provides a logical open air dining porch in summer, and the front porch could be enclosed with operating sash thus providing an "all year round" house for cold climes. Ample facilities are provided for the introduction of hedges, dwarfed trees and window flower boxes.

The bungalow at Robbins Point is on a rocky slope near the water's edge and is only intended for summer use. Between the massive stone piers there will be a heavy lattice, the space back of which will be used for storage purposes. The ground floor contains all of the bedrooms, though there is ample space in the large loft for any additional sleeping-room capacity which may be desired.

The living room and dining room are on opposite sides of the building with a wide opening between. There is a large fireplace in the living room and another big stone chimney contains the flues from the kitchen and laundry.

The porch runs almost around the building and the posts and rails are the natural trunks and branches of trees, not trimmed too close. The interior of the entire building is finished in stained wood, the ceilings are beamed, and all rooms open directly on the porch, as well as into one another.

The outside will weather to a natural gray which, combined with the natural effect of the porch and the rough stone work, will cause the building to blend into the landscape as seen from the water, its only means of approach.

The bungalow designed by Antonin Nechodoma for his own home at San Juan, Porto Rico, has walls built of reinforced concrete and a roof covered with real antique Spanish tile. All of the trim and the floors throughout are of solid Dominican mahogany, and the bungalow is consequently an expensive one, it having cost $10,000 to build.

_____

The site of the interesting bungalow shown on page 32 is unusual, as the building stands on two small, low, rocky islands near Gananoque, Ont.

One end of the building with the chimneys is built of rough pieces of Randon red granite. The other walls are covered with copper stained shingles, and the shingle roof and exterior trim are stained green. The principal floor overhangs the waterway between the two islands, giving a suitable boat house below, in which there is also the gas plant and a gasoline engine for pumping. Besides the three bedrooms on the main floor, there are three in the second story. The verandas are wide and roomy and flower boxes have been used effectively on the railings.

_____

The rambling roof lines and projecting eaves of the California bungalow, presented on page 33, are particularly attractive, with the broad span of the roof beams, battering porch columns and chimneys. The exterior is designed to be built of shakes spaced about three inches apart, which give a pleasing and rustic effect, harmonizing with the cobblestone work in the foundation, porch walls, columns and chimneys.

The door has a wrought-iron grille over the glass with an iron knocker below and is hung with large strap-iron hinges. The entrance is directly into the living room, which contains a fireplace occupying one end of the room with bookcases on each side.

The feature of the dining room is a buffet extending across the entire outside wall with a large plate glass observation window in the center and china closets with small hinged windows above on both sides. The living room and dining room have beamed ceilings. The house contains eight rooms and two bathrooms. There is an outdoor sitting room opening from one of the bedrooms, which, if so desired, can be screened and used as an outdoor sleeping porch. Two sides of the breakfast room are entirely enclosed with French windows, which open onto a spacious pergola.

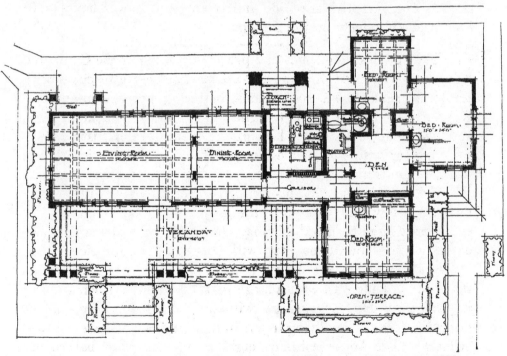

BUNGALOW FOR ANTONIN NECHODOMA, ARCHITECT, AT JUAN, PORTO, RICO.

(Described on page 28)

47

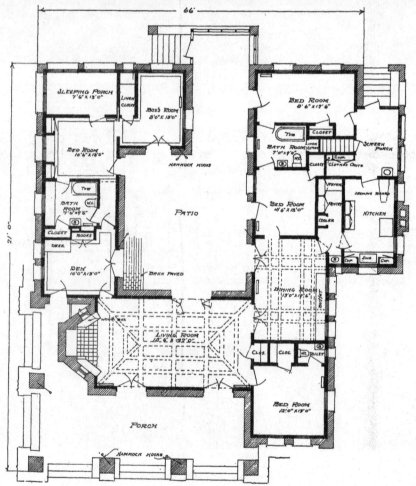

Robert H. Orr, Architect.

BUNGALOW AT POMONA, CAL.

Robert H. Orr, Architect.

BUNGALOW AT POMONA, CAL.

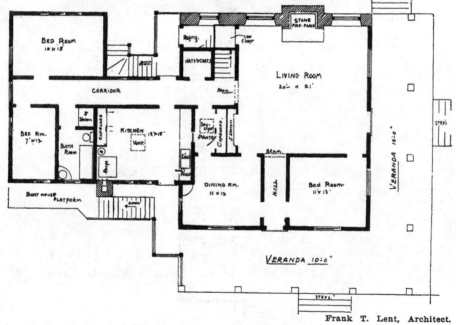

Frank T. Lent, Architect.

A BUNGALOW, THOUSAND ISLANDS, N. Y.

(Described on page 28)

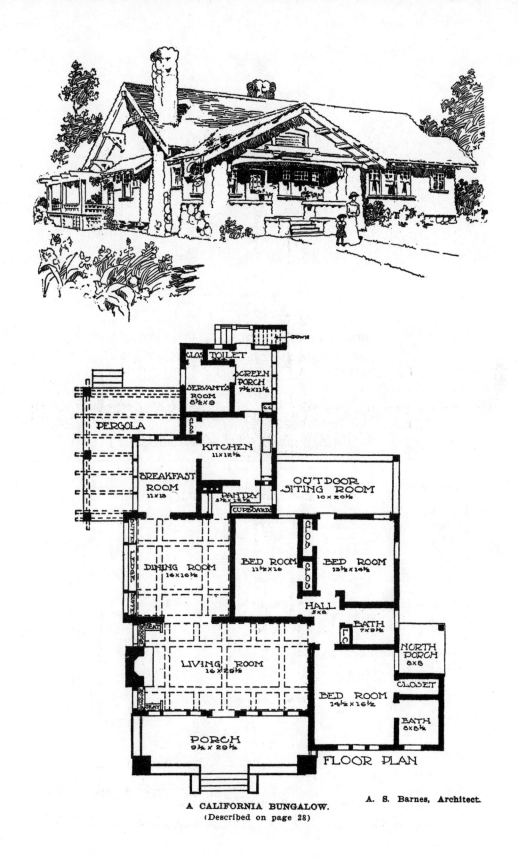

A CALIFORNIA BUNGALOW.
(Described on page 28)

A. S. Barnes, Architect.

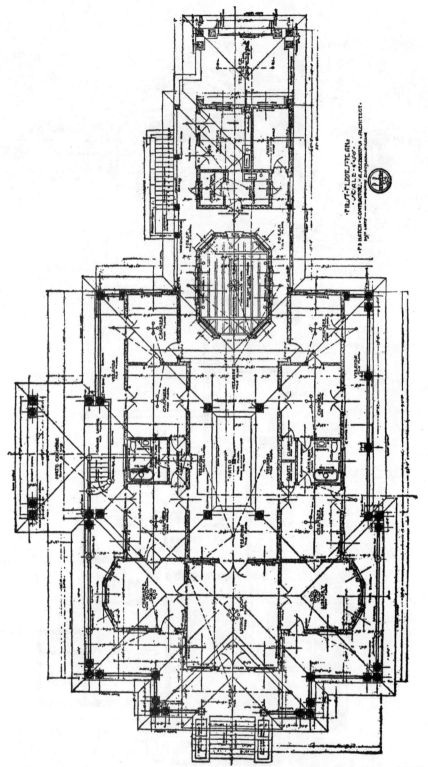

Antonin Nechodoma, Architect.

PLAN OF BUNGALOW AT SANTURCE, PORTO RICO.

Antonin Nechodoma, Architect.

BUNGALOW AT SANTURCE, PORTO RICO.

(Described on page 38)

Trost & Trost, Architects.

BUNGALOW AT EL PASO, TEXAS.

ANOTHER CALIFORNIA BUNGALOW

REDWOOD LOGS SUPPORT THE VERANDA OVERHANG.   SEVEN ROOMS.   COST $5,000.

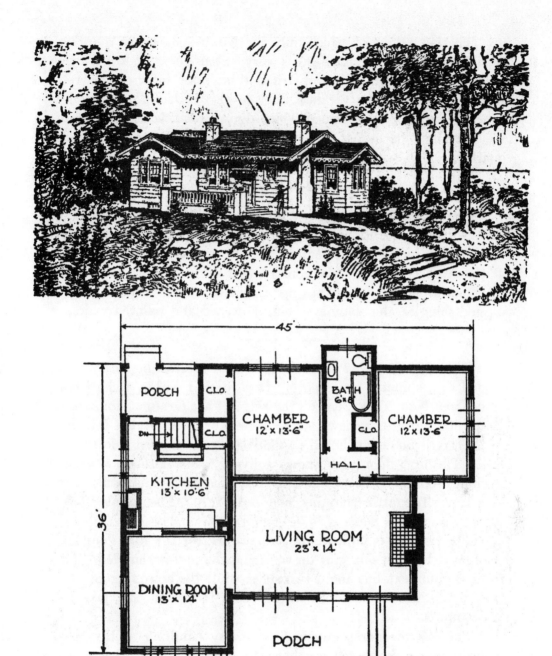

Labels within floor plan:

45

PORCH   CLO.

BATH
6"x8"

CHAMBER
12'x13'-6"

CHAMBER
12'x13'-6"

DN   CLO.

KITCHEN
13'x10'-6"

HALL

CLO.

36'

LIVING ROOM
23'x14'

DINING ROOM
13'x14'

PORCH

C. E. Schermerhorn, Architect.

"LAKESIDE BUNGALOW."   LARGE LIVING ROOM A FEATURE.

(Described on page 38)

The bungalow, of which only the front is shown in the illustration at the top of page 35 is very extensive as shown by the accompanying plan. The construction is frame built on concrete footings rising to the veranda floor level. It has a patio about which the rooms are grouped. The dining room is at the rear of the patio and beyond it in a wing are the kitchen and servants' quarters. The cost of this building was $22,000.

The "Lakeside Bungalow" on page 37 illustrates a rambling plan with an exceptionally well thought out scheme which produces a very pleasing and picturesque exterior, with a porch terrace at the front entrance. The construction is frame with very wide clapboards painted white, having chocolate brown trimmings and dipped shingles, the chimneys being stuccoed and painted white.

On pages 39 to 42 there is shown an interesting design, intended as a summer house only. It is located within a short distance from New York City, on the ridge of the Orange Mountains. Its position affords a view toward New York and Staten Island.

There is no cellar, but the foundations are carried below frost line. The first floor plan shows a living room, kitchen and two sleeping rooms. The veranda is intended to be used also for sleeping. The attic contains two bedrooms. The ample closet space in so small a house is to be commended.

The exterior is built of rough masonry for the first floor and chimney, while the siding of the attic and the roof is shingled. The front veranda extends about two sides, while the balcony above the back porch gives an outdoor sitting room facing another point of the compass.

The interior perspectives show a cosy handling of the main living room—a simple scheme that is the keynote of the other rooms of the bungalow.

As to the plumbing, a pump at the rear porch is thought sufficient to provide the water necessary in the kitchen and the bedrooms. The pump connects with a tank in the attic, from which the water closet is supplied. The cesspool is placed 15 feet back of the bungalow. The cost was $2,300 complete.

BAY WINDOW LIVING ROOM.   BUNGALOW, ORANGE MOUNTAINS, N. J.

F. G. Lippert, Architect.

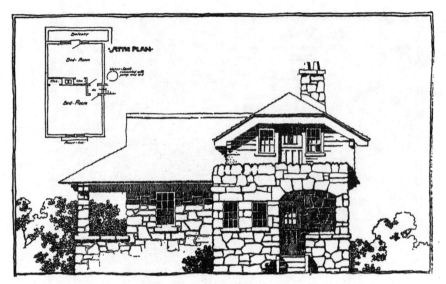

REAR ELEVATION.

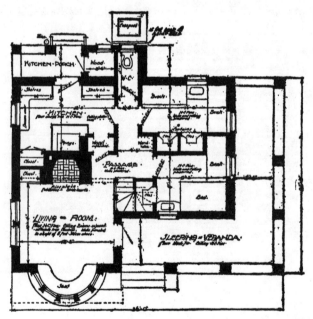

F. G. Lippert, Architect.

FIRST STORY PLAN.

FRONT ELEVATION.

SECTION
THROUGH PORCH CEILING.
Scale 1" = 1 Fd.

F. G. Lippert, Architect.

SIDE ELEVATION.

BUNGALOW ON THE RIDGE OF THE ORANGE MOUNTAINS, N. J.

(Described on page 38)

SKETCH OF THE LIVING ROOM.   BUNGALOW, ORANGE MOUNTAINS, N. J.

F. G. Lippert, Architect

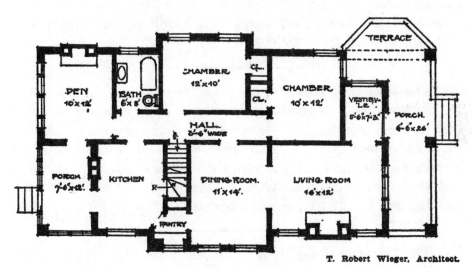

T. Robert Wieger, Architect.

A BUNGALOW DESIGN.

The plan of the farm bungalow was prepared by the United States Department of Agriculture; it is one of a series of plans for farm houses. This is intended as an inexpensive farm tenant house but it presents so many very excellent ideas and is so well studied that it will hold its own with many far more costly designs. To any one wishing to build a small bungalow its suggestions are most interesting. It is a small, four-cornered structure of one story without bay windows, gables or dormers or any projection save the overhanging roof to protect the walls and window openings. The house is planned to contain within the smallest dimensions and with the least expensive arrangement quarters to meet the needs and conveniences of a small family. It has but one chimney and one outside entrance and has no inside plumbing, except the water supply from the pump and a sink drain.

The problem of making one entrance serve for main and kitchen entrance is well solved. The working accommodations of the house are simple and direct and below the kitchen stove and fireplace there is an ash-pit large enough to take a year's supply and with clean out from the outside. A fuel box is also provided, large enough to take a week's supply; it is built in under the kitchen table and is filled from the outside.

The bungalow shown on page 47 was built at Wilmington, N. C., and has five rooms and bath. It is shingled all over with cypress shingles left to weather. Trimmings are painted white and blinds green. The interior woodwork in the living hall is stained a moss green and waxed, the walls are tinted in flat colors and there are brick mantels in all the rooms. The cost of the building was $1,327.50, the mantels extra.

The following design is very similar to the preceding one and was designed by the same architect. It gives a little different arrangement of rooms and is a little more expensively built. The method of heating is the same, that is, entirely by fireplaces, and the cost was $1,647.50, complete. Both of these designs are of simple plan which reduces the cost of construction. The same models could be finished in stucco to produce a very different design at a slight increase in cost.

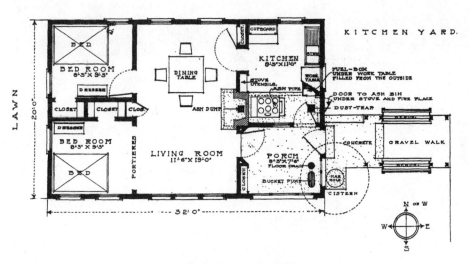

THE FARM BUNGALOW.
(Described on page 44)

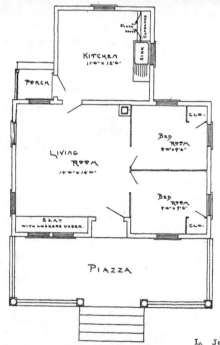

L. Jerome Aimar, Architect.

BUNGALOW AT NAVESINK HIGHLANDS, N. J.

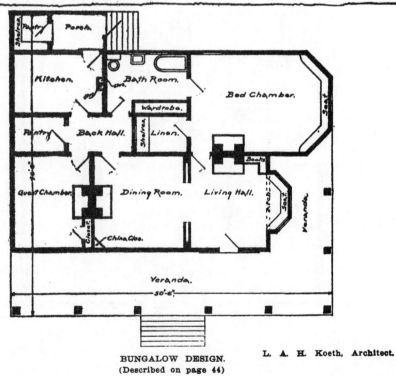

BUNGALOW DESIGN.
(Described on page 44)

L. A. H. Koeth, Architect.

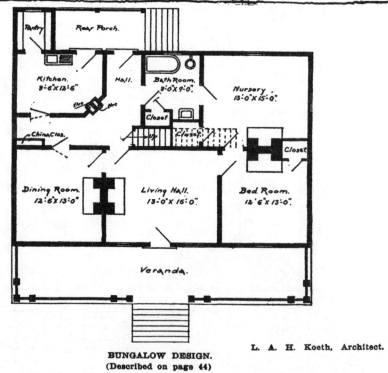

BUNGALOW DESIGN.
(Described on page 44)

L. A. H. Koeth, Architect.

66

Piazza
12' x 20'

Bed Rm
11' x 14'

Bed Rm
11' x 14'

Bed Rm
11' x 14'

Passage

Bath

Living Room
19' x 26'

Dining Rm
12' x 15'

Bed Rm
11' x 14'

Seats

Seat

Porch

Kitchen
12' x 14'

S Porch
6' x 10'

A SEVEN ROOM BUNGALOW.   George J. Webster, Architect.
(Described on page 53)

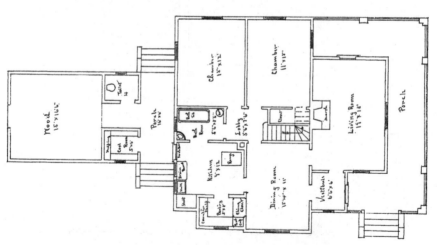

F. M. Starrett, Architect.

SUBURBAN BUNGALOW, FOREST GROVE, OREGON.
(Described on page 53)

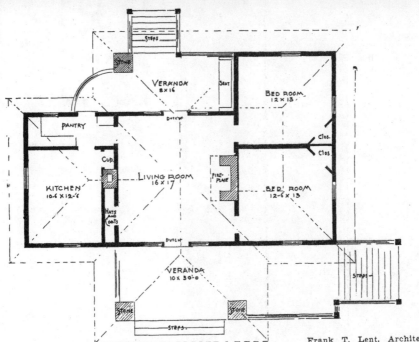

Frank T. Lent, Architect.

A THOUSAND ISLANDS BUNGALOW, ST. LAWRENCE RIVER, N. Y.
(Described on page 53)

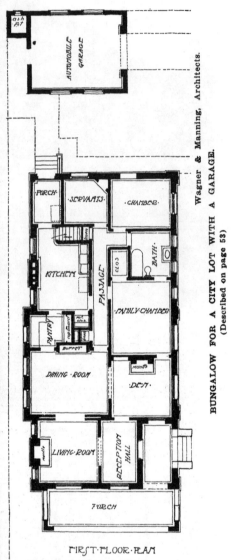

BUNGALOW FOR A CITY LOT WITH A GARAGE.

(Described on page 53)

Wagner & Manning, Architects.

FIRST·FLOOR·PLAN

The living room of the seven-room bungalow on page 49 has windows to the north, east and south, and on the south and east are large piazzas.

The dining room communicates directly with the kitchen and by closing one door leading to the passage all the bedrooms are isolated from the living apartments. The house has ten good-sized closets.

Both outside and inside are built and finished with California redwood, the exterior being covered with redwood shingles, stained a rich brown, while the interior is paneled in redwood and stained. There are built-in buffets with leaded glass doors, built-in seats and bookcases, also heavy beamed ceilings and a large open fireplace of cobblestones.

The bungalow at Forest Grove, Oregon, is built upon a concrete foundation with a shingle exterior finish. The interior trim is flat grain, steam-treated fir, finished with a wood filler and hard oil. In the second story there are three sleeping rooms in addition to those of the first story. The building cost about $2,500.

The bungalow on page 51 was built for $1,000, upon a rocky island some 50 feet above the waters of the St. Lawrence river. The features of the exterior are the rustic lichen-covered stone columns which carry the veranda roof. These with the stone foundation piers give the little place a strikingly substantial and permanent appearance. The living room is used as dining room as well and contains a weathered stone fireplace. There is also a kitchen and pantry and two fair-sized bedrooms.

The city bungalow shown on the opposite page occupies a corner lot 37½x125 feet. The exterior is faced with a gray pressed brick with white lava stone trimming all laid in white mortar. The shingle roof is stained a moss green. The interior trim throughout is red birch stained mahogany except the dining room and den, which are oak, quarter sawed, stained medium brown. All floors except in the rear part are quarter sawed oak. Bath and kitchen have tiled floors and wainscots and all plumbing is porcelain ware. The cost of building was $7,382.

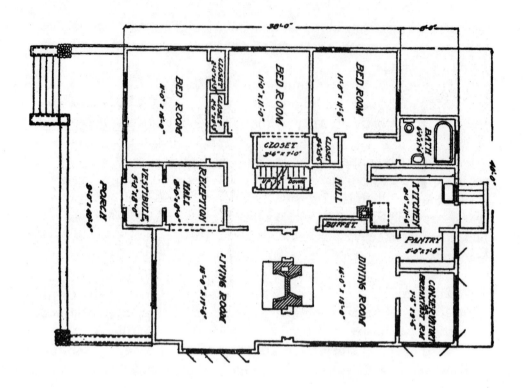

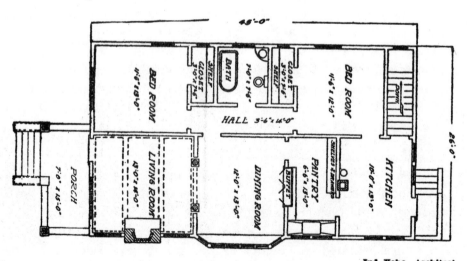

Jud Yoho, Architect.

FIVE AND SIX ROOM BUNGALOWS AT SEATTLE, WASHINGTON.

Jud Yoho, Architect.

FIVE AND SIX ROOM BUNGALOWS AT SEATTLE, WASHINGTON.

FIVE ROOM BUNGALOW AT SEATTLE, WASHINGTON.

BUNGALOW AT DELAWARE WATER GAP, PA.

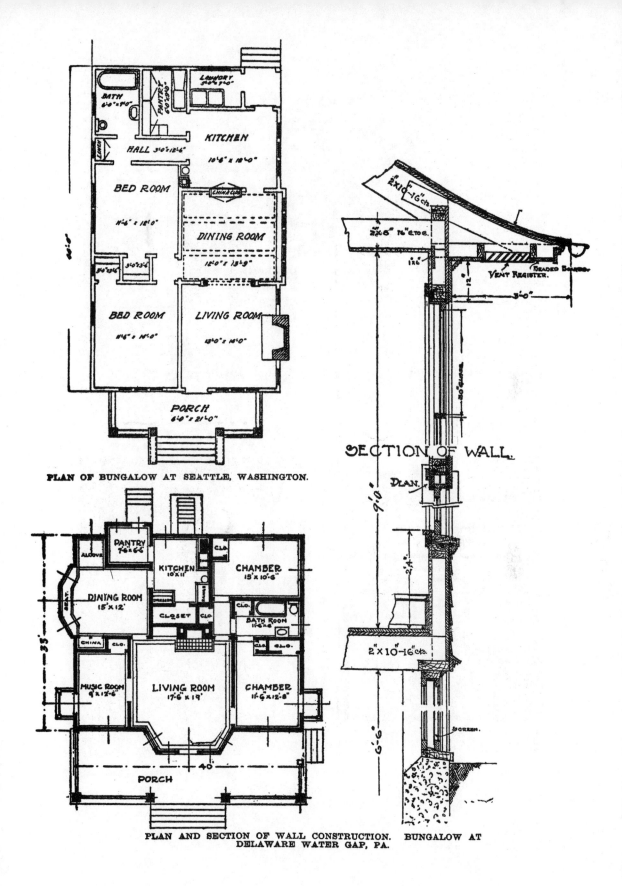

PLAN OF BUNGALOW AT SEATTLE, WASHINGTON.

SECTION OF WALL.

PLAN AND SECTION OF WALL CONSTRUCTION. BUNGALOW AT
DELAWARE WATER GAP, PA.

75

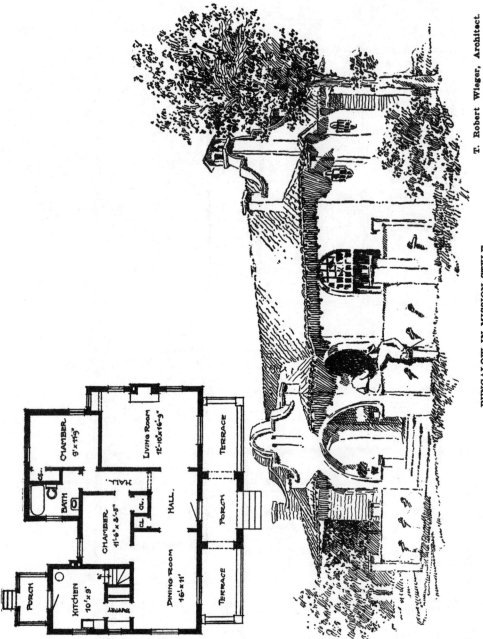

BUNGALOW IN MISSION STYLE.

T. Robert Wieger, Architect.

SKETCH OF BUNGALOW.   T. Robert Wieger, Architect.

77

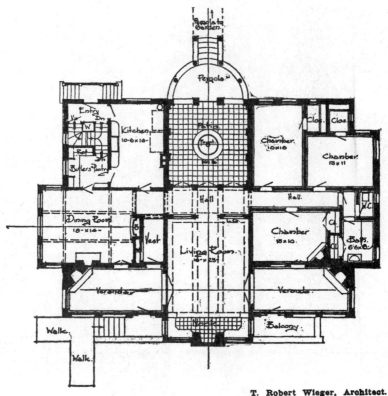

PLAN OF BUNGALOW ON PAGE 59.

The plan of the bungalow shown on page 63 provides a room for a maid, a den with sliding door which can be converted into an additional chamber should an emergency arise; a fascinating "ingle nook" in the living room with seat on either side of the large open fireplace, and in addition a roomy front porch and surrounding terrace. The terrace off the dining room is well suited for out-of-door dining..

The "Bungalow with Pergola Porch" on page 73 shows a most simple and direct plan, having a generous pergola porch, and space on the second floor to accommodate several additional rooms or a sleeping porch. It is constructed of hollow tile with stucco finish with shingle roof stained moss green. The walls are embellished with applied lattices for climbing vines.

BUNGALOWS IN PORTO RICO.   Antonin Nechodoma, Architect.

FIELD STONE FOR THE VERANDA BASE AND CHIMNEY.
A SOUTHERN CALIFORNIA BUNGALOW.

TERRACE INSTEAD OF VERANDA IN A BUNGALOW AT PASADENA, CAL.
SEVEN ROOMS.   COST $3,000.

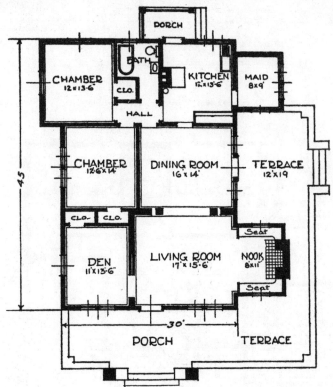

C. E. Schermerhorn, Architect.

A COMMODIOUS BUNGALOW.

(Described on page 60)

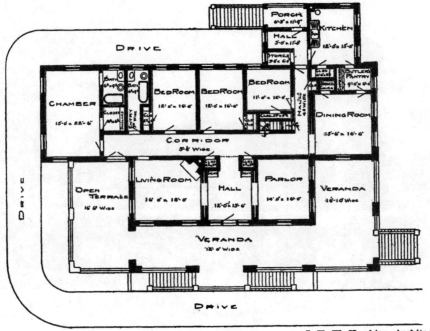

J. H. W. Hawkins, Architect.

BUNGALOW AT JACKSONVILLE, FLA.

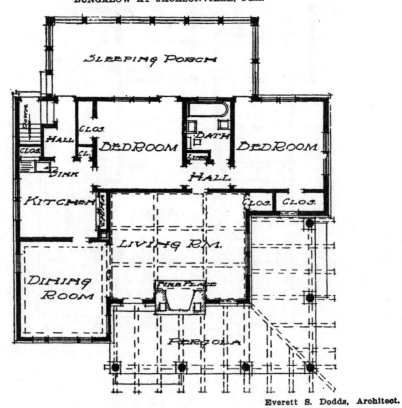

Everett S. Dodds, Architect.

BUNGALOW AT OMAHA, NEBRASKA.

J. H. W. Hawkins, Architect.

CONCRETE BLOCKS AND TILE ROOF.   A BUNGALOW AT JACKSONVILLE, FLA.

Everett S. Dodds, Architect.

BUNGALOW AT OMAHA, NEBRASKA.

THIS CALIFORNIA BUNGALOW COST $4,000.

A PATIO WITH A FOUNTAIN.   EIGHT ROOMS.   COST $4,000.

Arnott Woodroofe, Architect.

BUNGALOW BUILT OF EXPOSED HOLLOW TILE AT STEILACOOM LAKE, WASH.

C. W. Bulger & Sons, Architects.

BUNGALOW AT OAKLAWN, DALLAS, TEXAS.

Courtesy of "The Interlocker."

BUNGALOW AT EL PASO, TEXAS.

BUNGALOW AT TUCSON, ARIZONA.   Trost & Trost, Architects.

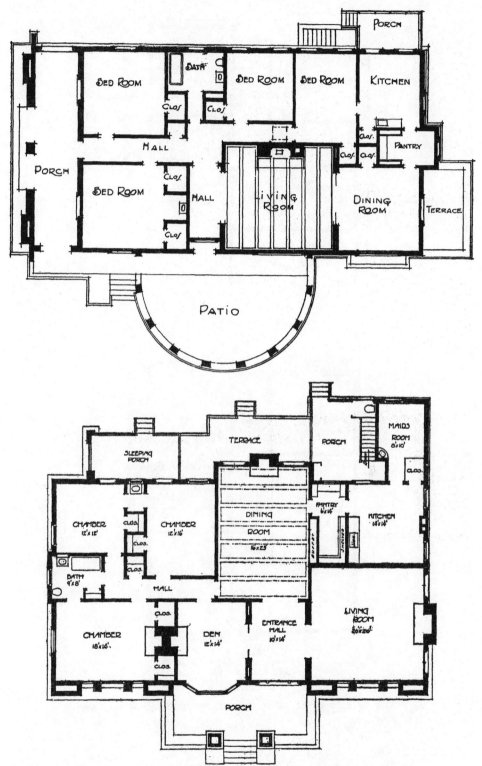

PLANS OF THE TWO BUNGALOWS ON THE OPPOSITE PAGE.

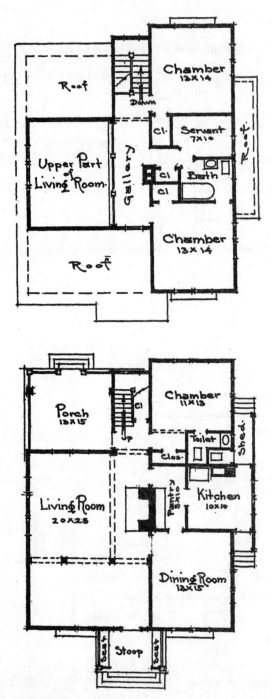

PLANS OF THE COTTAGE BUNGALOW ON THE OPPOSITE PAGE.

A COTTAGE BUNGALOW AT CAPE MAY, N. J.

A SHINGLE CABIN.

THIS RUSTIC LIVING ROOM HAS TWO WIDE FIREPLACES.

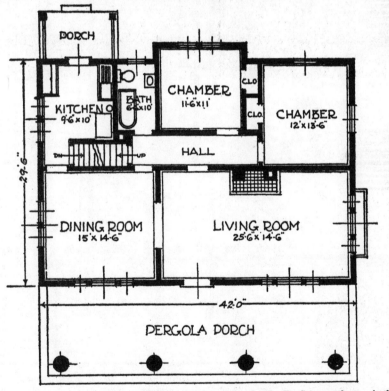

PORCH

KITCHEN
9'-6" x 10'

BATH
6'-6" x 10'

CHAMBER
11'-6" x 11'

CLO

CLO

CHAMBER
12' x 13'-6"

DN

UP

HALL

29'-6"

DINING ROOM
15' x 14'-6"

LIVING ROOM
25'-6" x 14'-6"

42'-0"

PERGOLA PORCH

C. E. Schermerhorn, Architect.

BUNGALOW WITH PERGOLA PORCH.
(Described on page 60)

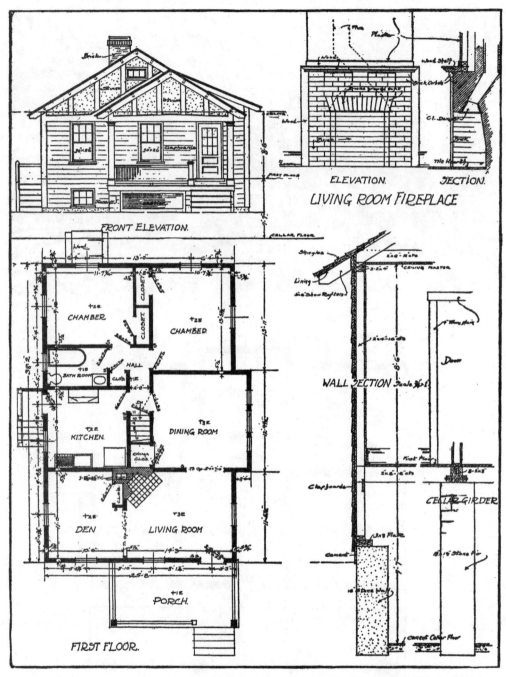

ELEVATION.   SECTION.

LIVING ROOM FIREPLACE

FRONT ELEVATION.

WALL SECTION Scale ½"=1'

CELLAR GIRDER

FIRST FLOOR.

C. E. Schermerhorn, Architect.

BUNGALOW AT BROOMALL, PA.

92

BUNGALOWS OF COTTAGE TYPE

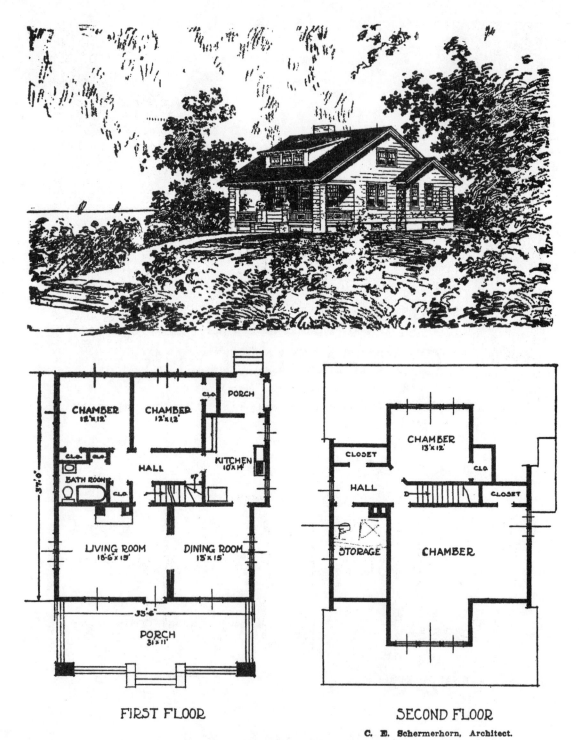

FIRST FLOOR

SECOND FLOOR

C. E. Schermerhorn, Architect.

SEVEN ROOM BUNGALOW OF COTTAGE TYPE.

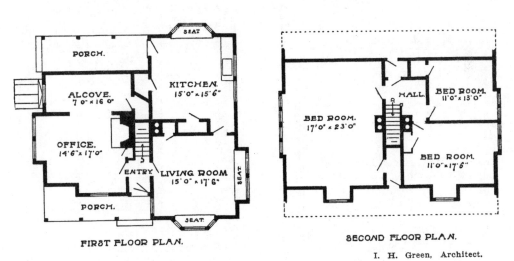

FIRST FLOOR PLAN.

SECOND FLOOR PLAN.

I. H. Green, Architect.

A GATE LODGE FOR AN ESTATE AT GREAT RIVER, N. Y.

95

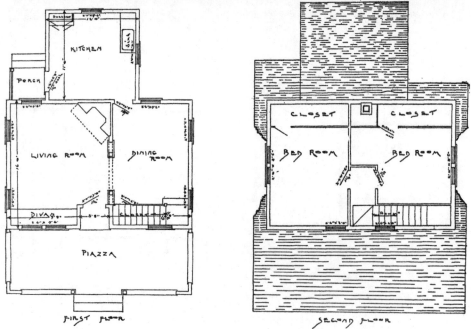

BUNGALOW OF L. JEROME AIMAR, ARCHITECT, NAVESINK HIGHLANDS, N. J.

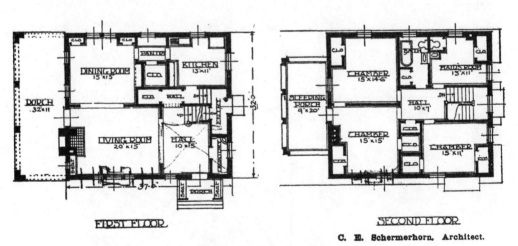

FIRST FLOOR

SECOND FLOOR

C. E. Schermerhorn, Architect.

HOUSE AT YARDLEY, PA.

The plan of "Maronook" at Leland, Mich., is laid out to accommodate an irregular piece of ground, which is a plateau overlooking Lake Leezanau. On account of the house being in close proximity to the embankment the drive or entrance front is at what would be rightly called the rear. This drive winds among the trees to the wide porch, which has large boulder piers at each corner. Extending upwards and flanking the steps of all the porches are piles of boulders laid up without mortar. The exterior of the house is built with boulder field stone and the woodwork is of rough siding stained seal brown. The trimmings around the windows, cornice and columns are painted ivory white. The roof projecting seven feet from the main wall of the building, is built with exposed rafters. The soffit of these eaves is of rough lumber, laid close and stained a russet yellow. The shingle work on the roofs and dormers is of a reddish brown, harmonizing well with the exterior siding. The boulder stone work is laid up without hammer or tool marks of any kind, the stones being put into place in their natural shape and laid so that the mortar joints do not show.

(*Continued on page 85*)

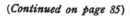

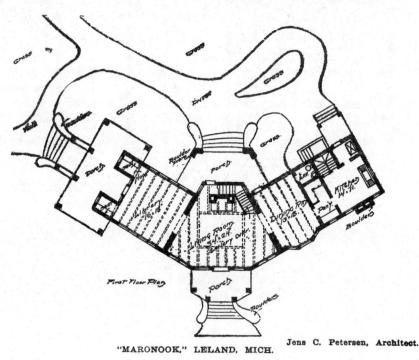

Jens C. Petersen, Architect.

"MARONOOK," LELAND, MICH.

"MARONOOK."   THE LAKE FRONT AND DRIVE APPROACH.

(Described on page 80)

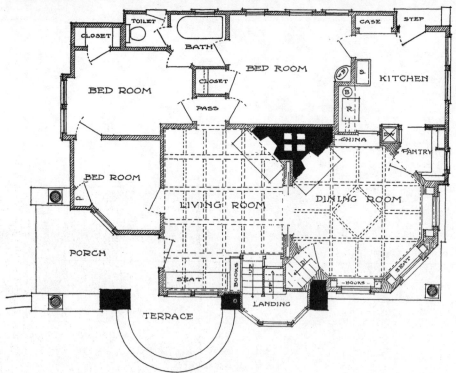

F. W. Reid, Architect.
COBBLE STONE AND SHINGLE.   A BUNGALOW AT PASO ROBLES, CAL.
(Described on page 85)

100

BUNGALOW AT PASO ROBLES, CAL.   F. W. Reid, Architect.

LIVING ROOM OF HOUSE AT POINT PARK, TENN.

(See pages 86-87)

D. V. Stroop, Architect.

The first floor living room, which is 34x24 feet, has an over gallery. A unique feature about this living room is the mammoth boulder stone fireplace which is ten feet across and extends to the ceiling. Circulating around it is the stairway leading to the sleeping rooms and the music room on the second floor. The interior of the house is finished with beamed ceilings and rough cast plaster, all of the woodwork and plaster being stained to harmonizing tones.

The building on pages 82-83 is erected on a hillside overlooking the town of Paso Robles and a stretch across thirty miles of the upper Salinas Valley. The exterior is built of cedar shingles left to weather on the walls and stained a grass green on the roof. The rough stone-work is a fossiliferous limestone, nearly white, and gathered from the nearby fields. In laying, pains had been taken to locate the stones for best artistic effect, and the joints are raked out to give the effect of a dry wall. The ceilings of porches and under the eaves are covered with Douglas slash grain fir, and varnished. The mouldings and window frames are painted bottle green. Inside finish is also of Douglas fir, selected slash grain and finished natural with a waxed surface. The living room and dining room are entirely finished in wood. The fireplace in the living room is faced with buff colored brick and the dining room fireplace is faced with a local rose granite. The basement is arranged to have a fireplace and space for two rooms and the attic has space for four rooms. The building cost $3,000, being done by day's work.

SHACK AT RAVEN ROCK, N. J.

Guy King, Architect.

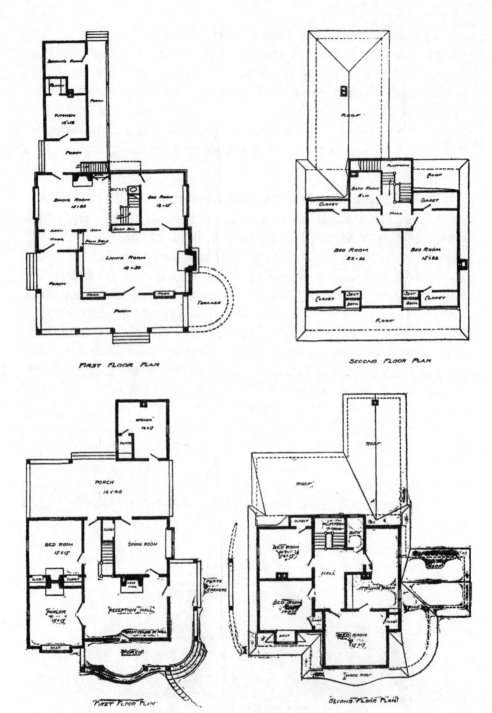

FIRST FLOOR PLAN

SECOND FLOOR PLAN

FIRST FLOOR PLAN

SECOND FLOOR PLAN

PLANS OF HOUSES ON THE OPPOSITE PAGE.

A SUMMER HOUSE AT POINT PARK, TENN.

ON THE CREST OF SIGNAL MOUNTAIN, TENN. D. V. Stroop, Architect.
(Described on page 90)

BUNGALOW AT SIGNAL MOUNTAIN, TENN.

TWO BUNGALOWS AT LOOKOUT MOUNTAIN, TENN.   D. V. Stroop, Architect.
(Described on pages 90-92)

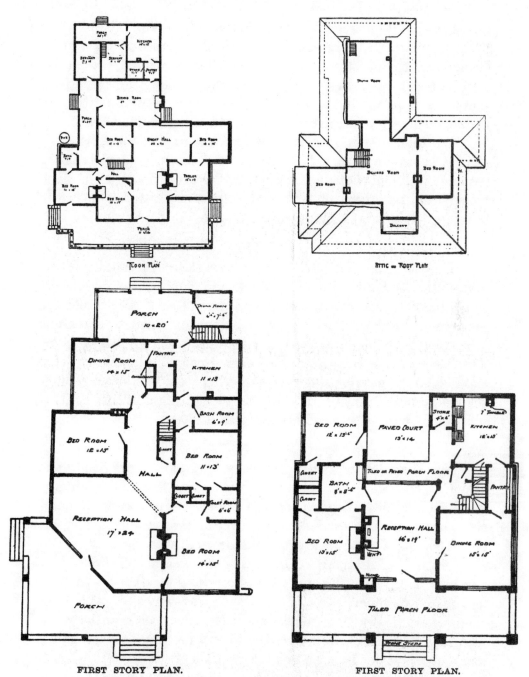

FLOOR PLAN

ATTIC or ROOF PLAN

FIRST STORY PLAN.

FIRST STORY PLAN.

PLANS OF THE **THREE BUNGALOWS** ON THE OPPOSITE PAGE.

The shingle finished house at Signal Mountain, Tenn. (page 87), is built of oak framing, storm sheathed, resting on a stone foundation, having stone veneer base of lichen covered and weathered surface rock carried to the level of the window sill belt entirely round the building. Above the base the walls as well as the roof are covered with hand rived chestnut oak shingles, stained.

The interior wood finish is of exposed dressed pine framing, stained brown, with panels of heavy terra cotta colored building paper. There is a stone fireplace in the reception hall of hand tooled local sandstone of pink and yellow variegated with brown veinings. It was built by day labor at a cost of $1,800.

The bungalow at Point Park, Lookout Mountain, Tenn. (page 87), is built of double plank and bonded wood walls on stone foundations, having a stone veneer base. The walls are papered and shingled with cypress shingles stained to a maroon brown and the gables are of the same shingles stained a rusty orange. The roof is of pine shingles stained moss green. The plank walls are exposed on the interior and stained bottle green, with beam ceilings stained tobacco brown. The fireplaces and mantels are built of weathered rough stones. The cost was $2,600.

The bungalow at the top of page 88 is on Signal Mountain, near Chattanooga. The construction is of pine framing, resting on stone foundations, with veneer and porch parapet walls of quarried local sandstone carried to the level of the parapet balustrade of the porch. The stones are hammer dressed, showing pink, yellow and brown variegations. The walls are weather boarded with 1x8 inch rough boarding, put on in horizontal weather-board fashion, mitred at corners and stained a tobacco brown color. The porch columns are of dead chestnut, stained the same color as the walls. The roof and gables are covered with cypress shingles, the gables and dormers stained brown and the roof silver gray.

The interior is of dressed local pine, finished with orange shellac, having panels between finished in burlap, worked out in different color schemes for various rooms. There are stone fireplaces of local sandstone hand tooled. The cost was $3,800, built by local day labor.

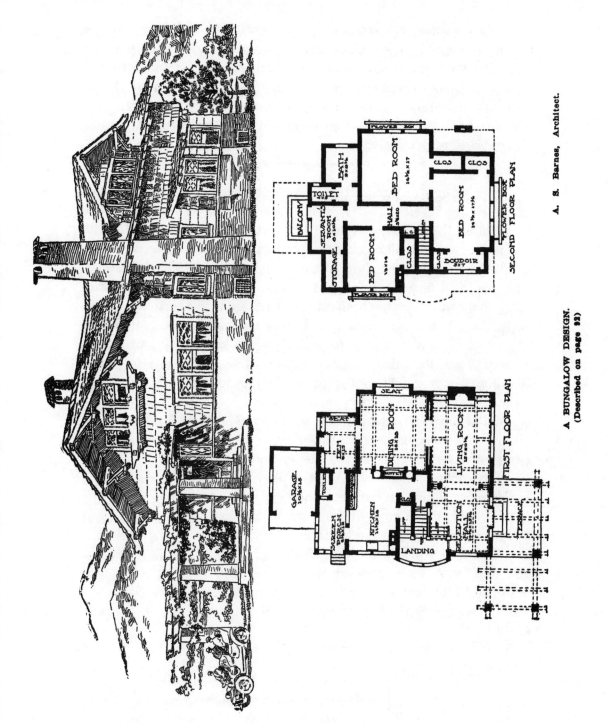

FLOWER BOX

BATH
6x9½

TOILET

BALCONY

SERVANTS
ROOM
6x10½

STORAGE

BED ROOM
13x14

HALL
9x20

BED ROOM
16½x17

CLOS

CLOS

CLOS

CLOS

CLOS

BED ROOM
14½x17½

BOUDOIR
5x7

FLOWER BOX

FLOWER BOX

SECOND FLOOR PLAN

A. S. Barnes, Architect.

SEAT

SEAT

DEN
9x13

DINING ROOM
16x16

BUFFET

LIVING ROOM
16x24

GARAGE
10x15

TOIL

KITCHEN
14x14

CLOS

SCREEN
PORCH

RECEPTION
HALL
14x14

LANDING

TERRACE

FIRST FLOOR PLAN

A BUNGALOW DESIGN.
(Described on page 92)

109

Two houses of bungalow type, each having rooms in the second story, are shown in the illustration at the bottom of page 88. The first story plan of each is shown on page 89. Their construction is balloon framing covered with a wire lathing and stucco. One has a shingle roof and the other a terra cotta tile roof. The interior finish of both is in pine, stained. They cost to erect, $2,100, and $3,200, respectively.

The design in perspective, shown on page 91, is very unusual but pleasing in effect. Its outline suggests the Swiss chalet and its details, the Mission style. The exterior is very simple with rough-cast cement plaster on the pergola columns and on the walls of the building to the height of the window sills, with shakes above, "Shakes" is a term used in California applied to large-sized, hand-split shingles. They are about one-half an inch thick, six inches wide, three feet long and are laid from twelve to sixteen inches to the weather, thus dividing the building into broad horizontal belts to accentuate the lines of a bungalow. The entire exterior finish is designed to be left in the rough to harmonize with the rough cement plaster and shakes.

The house is designed to admit all the light and sunshine possible, the pergola being substituted, with a small shelter over the front entrance, in place of the customary covered porch.

The house contains a reception hall with spacious stairway, a living room, dining room, den, kitchen, and screened porch in the first story; and four bedrooms, bath and balcony in the second story. There is a garage attached.

The woodwork in the reception hall, living room, dining room and den, with their paneled wainscoting and beamed ceilings is designed to be stained a very dark color, with dark rich tones on the walls, which, with the broad windows, gives a very cheery and cozy effect.

While the building on page 94 can hardly be called a bungalow, it possesses, nevertheless, bungalow attributes. It is two stories in height, built entirely of reinforced concrete, following the mission style, with a roof of red asbestos shingle. It cost to build $17,000.

LIVING ROOM, BUNGALOW AT SIGNAL MOUNTAIN, TENN.   D. V. Stroop, Architect.

(See pages 88-89)

Antonin Nechodoma, Architect.

TWO STORY HOUSE OF BUNGALOW TYPE, AT FAJARDO, PORTO, RICO.
(Described on page 92)

LOG HOUSES.

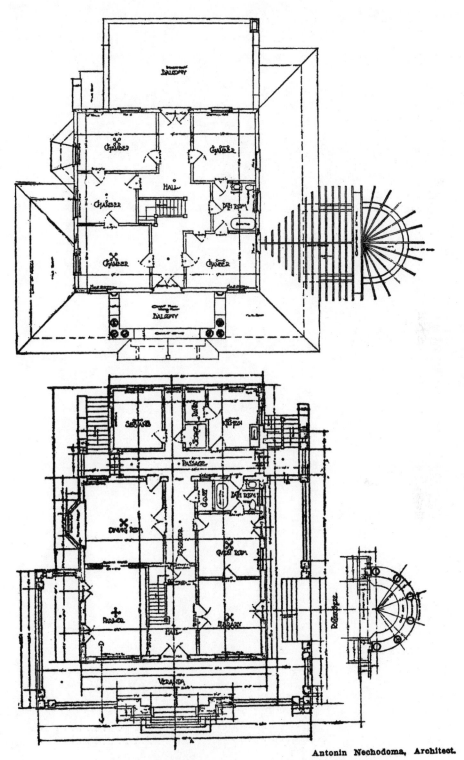

Antonin Nechodoma, Architect.

PLANS OF TWO STORY HOUSE AT FAJARDO, PORTO RICO.

CAMPS, LODGES
LOG CABINS

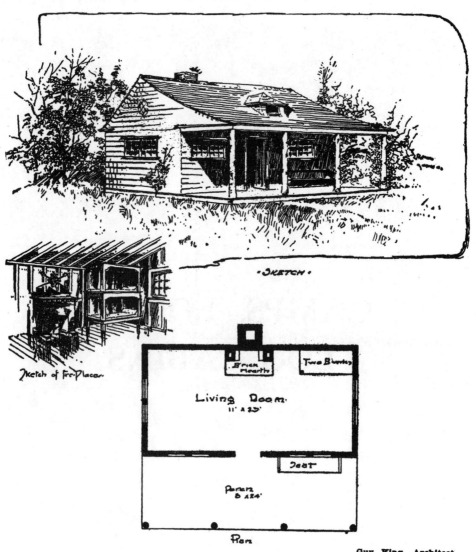

Sketch

Sketch of Fire-Place

Guy King, Architect.

SINGLE ROOM CABIN AT CHAPPAQUIDDICK, MASS.

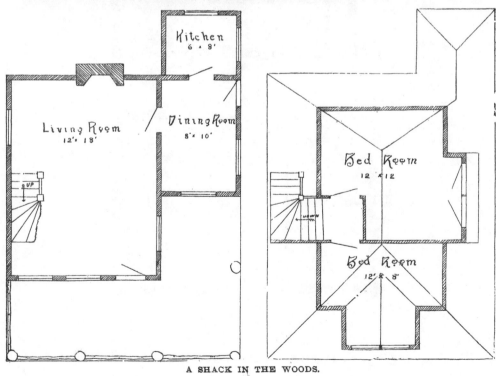

A SHACK IN THE WOODS.

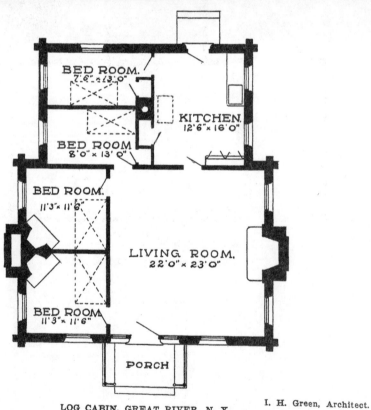

LOG CABIN, GREAT RIVER, N. Y. I. H. Green, Architect.

Floor plan labels:

BED ROOM.
7'6" × 13'0"

KITCHEN.
12'6" × 16'0"

BED ROOM
8'0" × 13'0"

BED ROOM.
11'3" × 11'6"

LIVING ROOM.
22'0" × 23'0"

BED ROOM
11'3" × 11'6"

PORCH

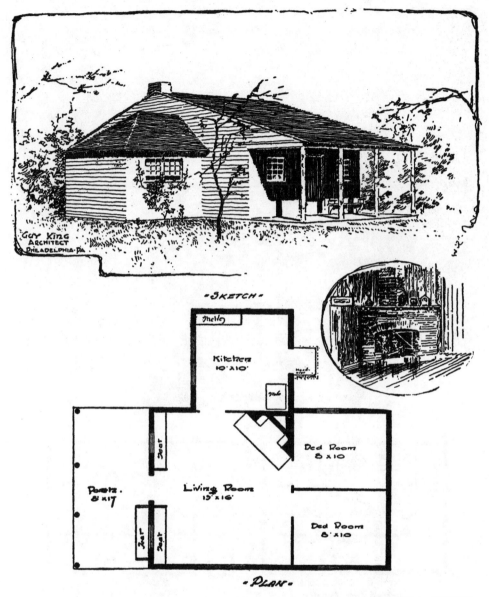

CABIN AT CHAPPAQUIDDICK, MASS.

Guy King, Architect.

First Floor Plan

Second Floor Plan

Guy King, Architect.

LOG CAMP, BLUE RIDGE MOUNTAINS, VA.

"Ashantee" (pages 105-106), that is the new part, is 18x27 feet. It is built on cedar posts, giving a cellar and good ventilation underneath. There are no floor joists, but instead 3 inch yellow pine plank laid flat and splined with heavy paper over them. This is covered with a good yellow pine floor. The side walls are built with 2 inch by 4 inch studs left rough and boarded outside with 7/8 inch by 6 inch hemlock which is papered and shingled. The exterior is painted dark green in harmony with the surrounding foliage. The roof, which is built at an angle of 45 degrees, boarded and shingled, is silver gray.

The exterior newel posts, hand rails and arbors are all built of twisted and gnarled swamp laurel, making a superb place for vines of all descriptions, especially wisteria and crimson ramblers.

In the interior the studs are left unfinished, which makes plenty of space for shelf room throughout and the woodwork was given one coat of old English wax stain and nothing else. The fireplace is constructed of rough arch bricks with 1 inch joints and an old railroad tie is used for mantel shelf. The hearth is 6 feet wide and runs the entire width of the house (18 feet). The brick work, both elevations of the fire place and hearth, have Mercer tile inserts at interesting points. The bed rooms contain bunks, each wide enough for two, with space above to build a double decker (on the steamer plan) if desired.

The log camp at White Bluffs, Tenn., shown on pages 110-111, was built for a summer house. The walls are built of spruce logs selected and seasoned to retain the bark without, but hand scraped to make a suitable inside finish. They are carefully laid and joined so as to show no tool or axe marks. Some rooms are plaster finished by nailing metal lath to the logs and plastering. The joints of the exterior are closed with black mortar scratched to give a shadow effect; within the joints of the scraped logs are closed with tinted mortar. Red cedar slabs are used for the doors and red cedar shingles for the roof. The porch is built from cedar poles and the ceiling of the porch and roof are built with cedar poles, making a beam finish. The half story above the first is lighted and ventilated by wide dormer windows at either end and consists of one large room used as a dormitory. The cost of building was $1,800.

The lodge at Stonecliffe, Me., shown on pages 117-118, is located at the juncture of a rock ledge and a sandy beach. The outlooks are planned to take in the magnificent ocean view. Internally, the living room is galleried 17 feet high at the middle, with the bedrooms at each end of the gallery. The structure is a guests' auxiliary for an adjoining cottage, there being no dining arrangements for the bungalow. The place, however, could be readily modified by parting off a dining room and kitchen at the westerly or fireplace end. The cost of the building thus finished may be reckoned about $5,000 without a cellar and founded on trench walls. Excavated and concreted cellar and furnace heating will add about $1,000 to this cost. A bathroom could be placed where the toilet now is shown on the gallery plan. In the Stonecliffe layout, which is only for summer use, there is a special bathhouse with three bathrooms supplied from the windmill waterworks system of the estate. This, and the beach bathing serve. Inside, the floor and walls of the bathhouses are tiled.

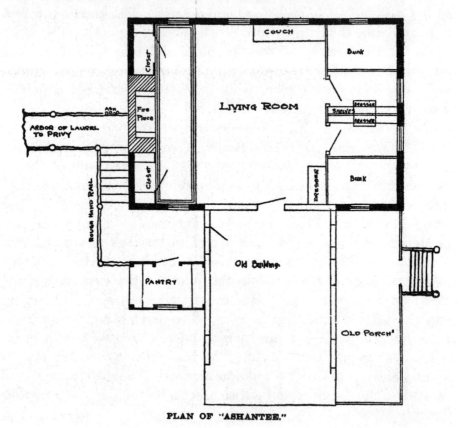

PLAN OF "ASHANTEE."

(Described on page 103)

C. E. Schermerhorn, Architect.

CAMP NEAR BETHLEHEM, PA.

124

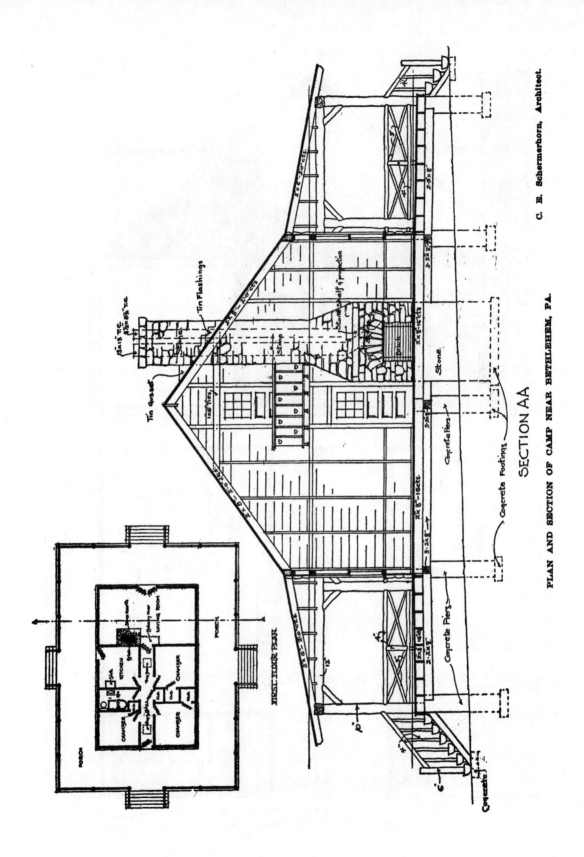

SECTION AA

PLAN AND SECTION OF CAMP NEAR BETHLEHEM, PA.

C. E. Schermerhorn, Architect.

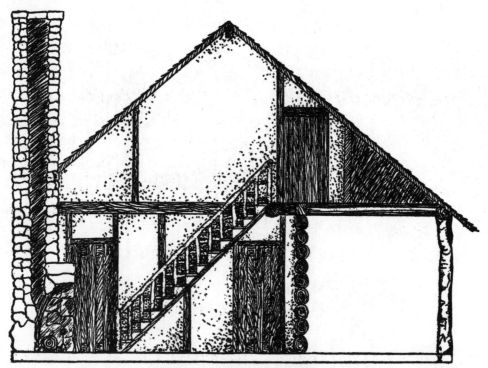

SECTION THROUGH LIVING ROOM.

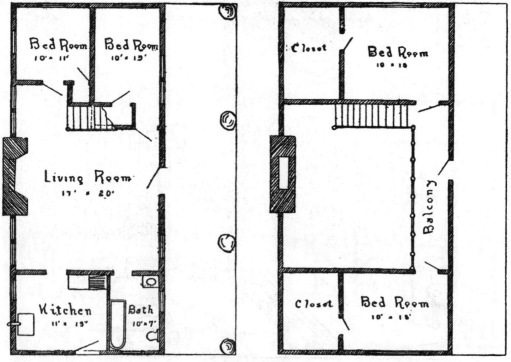

Bed Room
10' × 11'

Bed Room
10' × 15'

Living Room
17' × 20'

Kitchen
11' × 15'

Bath
10' × 7'

Closet

Bed Room
10' × 15'

Balcony

Closet

Bed Room
10' × 15'

PLAN SUGGESTIONS.

126

J. Calvin Stevens, Architect.

LOG HOUSE DESIGN.

SUGGESTION FOR A LIVING ROOM.

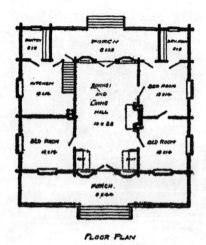

FLOOR PLAN

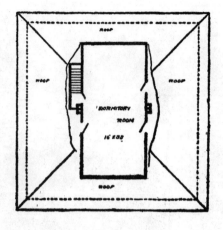

ROOF AND ATTIC PLAN

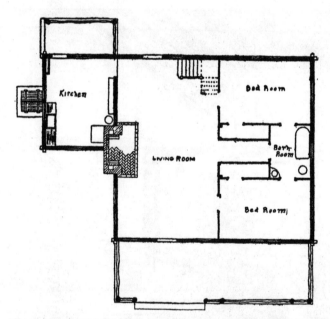

PLANS OF THE TWO LOG HOUSES ON THE OPPOSITE PAGE.

LOG CAMP AT WHITE BLUFFS, TENN.   D. V. Stroop, Architect.
(Described on page 103)

"HUNNEQUER'S QUEST," AT BROWN'S MILLS, N. J. Guy King, Architect.

C. E. Schermerhorn, Architect.

"MINNEWAWA," A RUSTIC LODGE AT BLUE MOUNTAIN LAKE, N. Y.

E. G. W. Dietrich, Architect.

LODGE AT LAKE PLACID, N. Y.

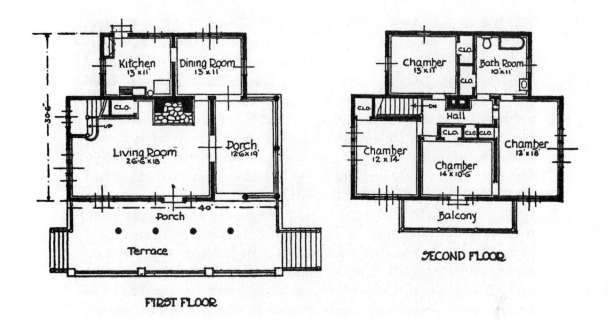

FIRST FLOOR

Kitchen 13'x11'

Dining Room 13'x11'

CLO.

UP

Living Room 26'6"x18'

Porch 12'6"x19'

Porch

Terrace

30'-6"

40'

SECOND FLOOR

Chamber 13'x11'

CLO.

Bath Room 10'x11'

CLO.

CLO.

Hall

CLO. CLO. CLO.

Chamber 12'x14'

Chamber 14'x10'6"

Chamber 12'x18'

Balcony

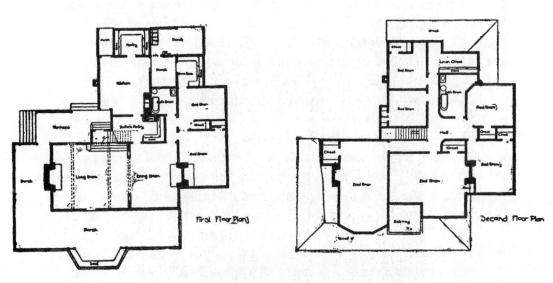

First Floor Plan

Second Floor Plan

PLANS OF THE LODGES ON THE OPPOSITE PAGE.

The Adirondack camp on Lake Wilbert, Franklin County, N. Y., shown on pages 121-123, is located on an ideal site on the shores of the lake. The whole estate is composed of 5,000 acres of woodland and entirely surrounds the lake. The location selected for the camp is on the west shore and is a knoll projecting well into the lake. The main lodge is about thirty feet above the lake and contains the living rooms and sleeping quarters, but the dining room and servants' quarters are in a separate building, about 200 feet from the main lodge, and are on a rocky point projecting into the lake and about 20 feet above the water. The connection between the two is by a covered rustic passage. Much care was taken to keep all the buildings, which include this dining room and boathouse, in addition to the main building in keeping with the surroundings, and not destroy, in their erection, the trees and shrubs surrounding them. The effort has been made to maintain the original state of the woods, and no attempt at landscape gardening was made in the surroundings.

Spruce logs ten inches in diameter, from which the bark was peeled, were used in the construction of the building, the spaces between are filled with Portland cement on a backing of wire lathing. The cement is light in color, while the logs and rustic work are stained with a rich brown wood preservative, giving the building a log cabin effect.

In the main lodge is a living room 25x40 feet, eight bedrooms, a gun room, five bathrooms and abundant closet rooms. In all the rooms rough stone fireplaces are provided. The living room, a view of which is given herewith, is the principal feature of the camp. At one end is a rustic staircase and at the other a massive stone fireplace; in the ceiling are massive hewn beams, with edges champhered, showing the axe marks. The panels between the studs are filled in with burlap. All exposed woodwork is stained a dark brown. The lighting is by acetylene gas, which by the use of glass chimneys and mica shades, is made to appear like kerosene lamps.

The dining room referred to above as being in a separate building, is an octagonal room 25 feet in width and open to the roof; a large open fireplace is opposite the entrance. A large dining room veranda overlooking the lake is at the end of the passage from the main lodge, which in favorable weather may be used for serving meals.

In the bedrooms, the walls and ceilings are finished in native spruce paneled and stained in a variety of soft colors. Casement windows are used throughout with the glass set in small panes. The long broad verandas, a good idea of which may be gained by the accompanying cut, form one of the chief attractions of the camp.

As the modern camp is at times a resort in winter, this building has been prepared for winter as well as summer use. The logs are covered with heavy building paper and sheathed with seven-eighth inch boards inside. Double sash are provided for all the windows and special care was taken to protect the plumbing from the cold.

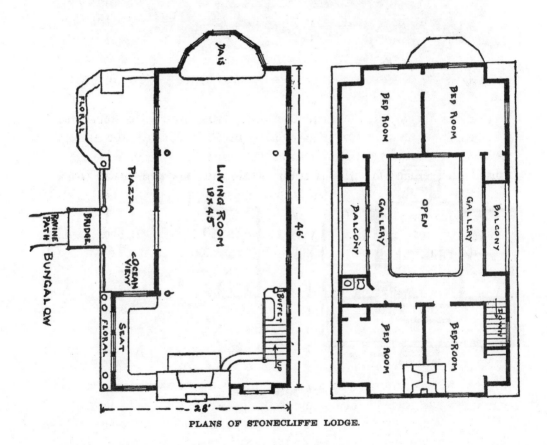

PLANS OF STONECLIFFE LODGE.

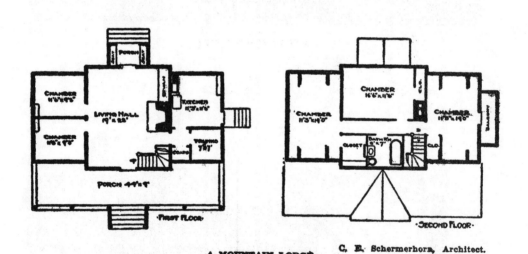

A MOUNTAIN LODGE.

C. E. Schermerhorn, Architect.

A SLAB SIDED LODGE.

Albert Winslow Cobb, Architect.

LODGE AT STONECLIFFE, MAINE.

(Described on page 104)

Albert Winslow Cobb, Architect.
IN THE LIVING ROOM AT STONECLIFFE, MAINE.

C. E. Schermerhorn, Architect.

PIAZZA AND DINING PORCH AT "MINNEWAWA."

Seymour & Schonewald, Architects.

CAMP AT LAKE TACONIC.

138

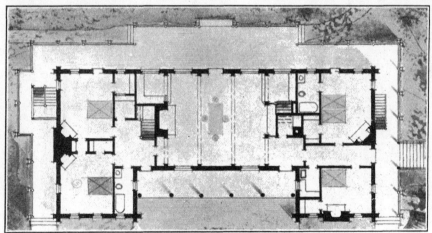

Davis, McGrath & Shepard, Architects.

AN ADIRONDACK CAMP.

(Described on page 114)

LIVING ROOM IN AN ADIRONDACK CAMP.   Davis, McGrath & Shepard, Architects.

Davis, McGrath & Shepard, Architects.

BEDROOM AND PIAZZA.   AN ADIRONDACK CAMP.

CAMP AT LAKE WAWAYANDA, SUSSEX CO., N. J.

LOG HOUSE AT LAKE WINOLA, PA.

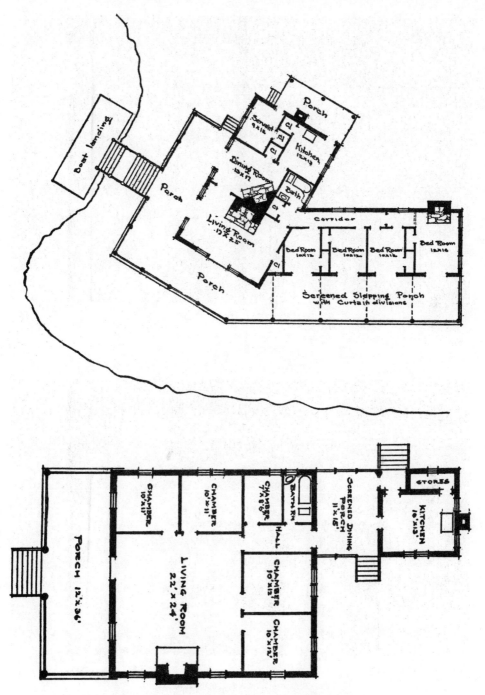

PLANS OF THE TWO CAMPS SHOWN OPPOSITE.